PUTNEY AND ROEHAMPTON IN 1665

A STREET DIRECTORY AND GUIDE

Dorian Gerhold

The British Academy Hearth Tax Project
Roehampton University London

(Occasional Historical Paper 1)

and

Wandsworth Historical Society

(Wandsworth Paper 16)

Acknowledgements: I am grateful to the following for permission to reproduce illustrations: Bodleian Library, 16; British Library (Crach 1.Tab.1.b.1, vol. XX), 8; Michael Bull, cover picture, col. plate 5, 10, 15, 20, 39, 44, 51; © Devonshire Collection, Chatsworth, reproduced by permission of Chatsworth Settlement Trustees, 24; Lord Feversham, col. plate 1; Fondation Custodia (collection F. Lugt), Institut Néerlandais, Paris, 17; Dorian Gerhold, 5, 14, 47; Peter Gerhold, 35; Guildhall Library, London, 27; Lady Hamilton of Dalzell, col. plate 7, col. plate 8; Lambeth Archives, 7, 12, 18, 23, 31; Lambeth Palace Library, 28; London Metropolitan Archives and St Mary's Parochial Church Council, Putney, 30; Merton Library and Heritage Service, 37; Museum of London, col. plate 2, 6; National Archives, 3; Northamptonshire Record Office, 50; Ordnance Survey, 54; Charles Pettiward, col. plate 4, col. plate 6; St Mary's Parochial Church Council, Putney, col. plate 3, 2, 4, 9, 32, 48, 52, 55; Jim Slade, 21; Wandsworth Local History Service, 1, 11, 43; Brian L. Wood (see below), 26, 29, 45, 46. Figs. 13, 19, 22, 25, 33, 34, 36, 38, 40, 41, 42 and 49 are from the Olney Collection, copies from which are held in Wandsworth Museum and Wandsworth Local History Service. I am particularly grateful to Michael Bull for extensive advice on illustrations and helping to locate them, and to Neil Robson for giving helpful advice on the arrangement of the text.

Figs. 26, 29, 45 and 46 are photographs taken for Project Matrix by Brian L. Wood, to whom the copyright belongs. Further information about these photographs and Project Matrix, a new county-wide Surrey Museums coin and token database, can be obtained from Surrey History Centre, Woking (tel: 01483 594624).

Note on money: One pound (£1) was divided into 20 shillings (20s.), which were each divided into 12 pennies (12d.).

Cover picture: View of St Mary's church, Putney, from Lower Richmond Road in about 1820. The overhanging building on the right is the one shown in Fig. 49.

ISBN – 978 0 905121 19 2

Contents

Appendices

Fig. 1. Putney's riverside, seen from the bridge in about 1750 (based on the painting reproduced here as colour plate 2). To the right of the church and the trees is the Red Lion Inn (probably rebuilt since 1665). To its right were the white buildings in Fig. 49 before they were altered, with four gables. The other buildings were on the riverside north of Lower Richmond Road: from left to right, the probable successor to No. 28; the Eight Bells and other buildings (about No. 26); a building with two gables which was part of Webb's Wharf (Nos. 20A to 23C); a building with three gables, some or all of which was later the Star and Garter (possibly Nos. 10-11). Despite the bridge (built in 1729) and improved roads, the old ferry landing at the foot of the High Street evidently remained a busy place.

Foreword

It is a great pleasure to introduce Putney and Roehampton in 1665. *Readers follow in the footsteps of the tax assessor, street by street and building by building, among both rich and poor, to acquire 'a more detailed view of Putney and its people than is possible for any other year before the censuses of 1841 onwards'. Dorian Gerhold's rich description of everyday life captures the imagination, ranging from those who served the Countess Dowager of Devonshire in Roehampton Great House, with its 350-acre park (part of which now forms the site of Roehampton University) to the working lives of the Thames watermen, and more tragically to the plague victims living out their last days in the pesthouses, specially built in 1665.*

By matching up the hearth tax returns with parish and other records and contemporary and later maps, Gerhold provides readers with a treasure trove of information on Putney and Roehampton at a time when the suburb was playing its role in the transformation of London from a medieval city to a modern metropolis. Moreover, the 'Directory of householders' in Part II is an invaluable source for local and family historians and for anyone interested in patterns of employment, wealth and poverty in this area in the past, with the employment pattern, as readers will discover, giving Putney a distinctive sound. Gerhold's comprehensive empirical account of the hearth tax data for Putney and Roehampton in 1665, with its narrative, tables, images and maps, will be greatly valued by all those with an interest in the area's history as well as those interested in the later Stuart age, and contributes to the work of the Hearth Tax Project and the Wandsworth Historical Society. I am pleased to recommend it to readers in the neighbourhood and beyond.

Andrew Wareham M.A., Ph.D., F.R.Hist.S.
Director, British Academy Hearth Tax Project, Roehampton University

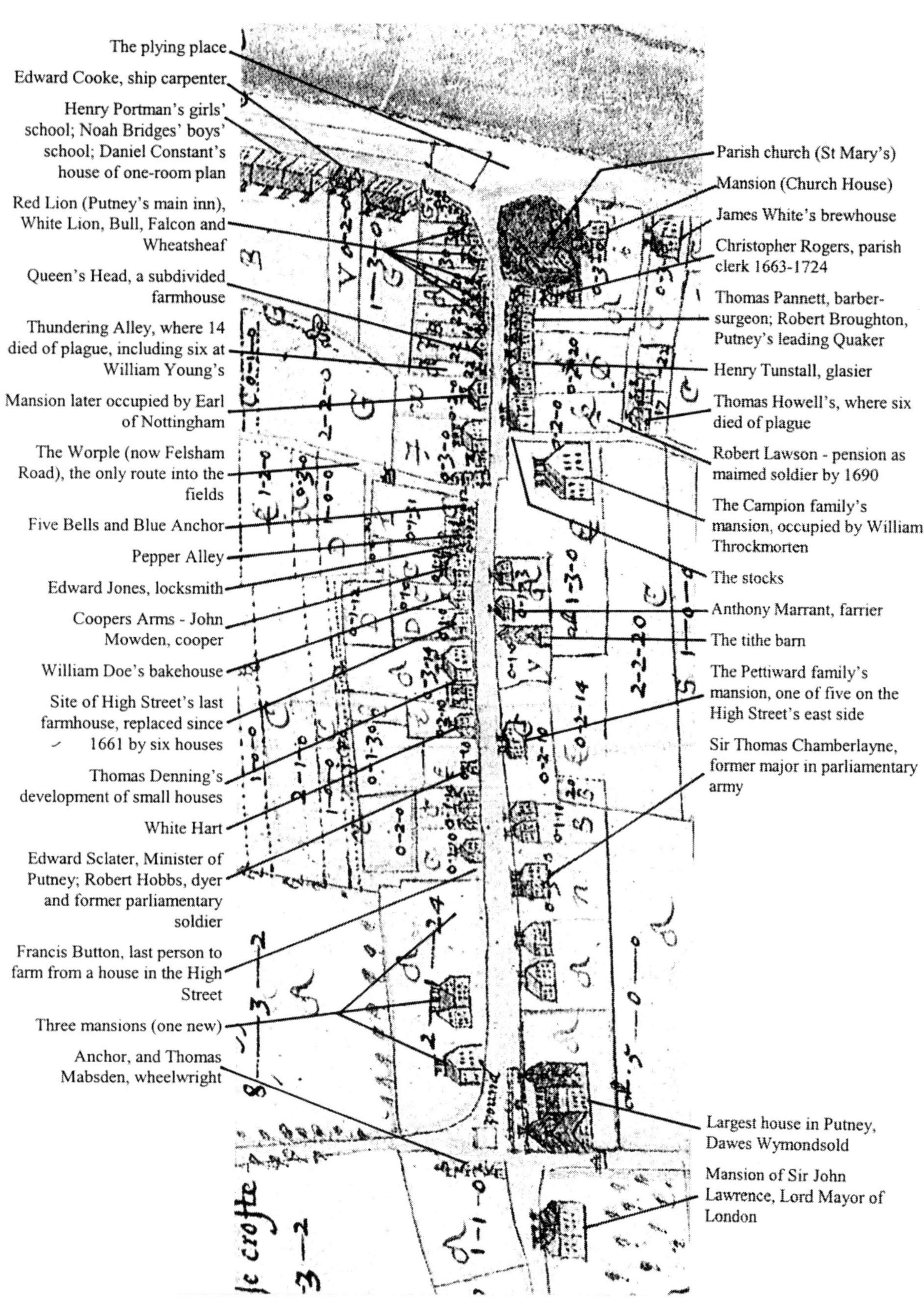

Fig. 2. Places of interest in and around Putney High Street in 1665, marked on the map of 1636. North is at the top of the page.

Part I

Putney and Roehampton in 1665

1. The hearth tax and its records

From 1662 to 1689 an unusual property tax was levied: it varied according to the number of hearths, or fireplaces, in each dwelling. One shilling was payable per hearth twice a year. It was of course highly unpopular, especially as petty constables were given the right to search houses to check the number of hearths declared: in 1663, when Putney's collector, Robert Lewis (No. 183 in the list below) tried to inspect the house of Owen Cooke (No. 192) at the lower end of the High Street, he was assailed by a cry of 'What! Do you come to robbe my house ... and you intende to steale my dishe', following which Cooke and his wife were successfully prosecuted for 'opprobrious words'.[1]

For the historian the great virtue of the hearth tax was that it resulted in lists of householders and their hearths. Although the lists provide only names and numbers, they are among the most important sources for studying seventeenth-century communities, because they cover all or nearly all householders and provide a rough indication of their prosperity and of the social structure of communities. Copies of the lists had to be sent to the Exchequer, and many of them have survived in the National Archives.

A relatively large number of lists exists for Putney parish. As elsewhere, they vary in character. Some omit the poorest householders (who were exempt), are incomplete in other ways, record the exempt and chargeable separately or place all the wealthier householders together at the start of the list. Fortunately, Peter Rogers, gardener or labourer, who compiled the list for Putney in or about April 1665,[2] recorded everyone in house-by-house order, from the pauper with one hearth to Dawes Wymondsold with 37 hearths (Fig. 3).[3] His list, which is set out in Part II below, is the single most informative document about seventeenth-century Putney.

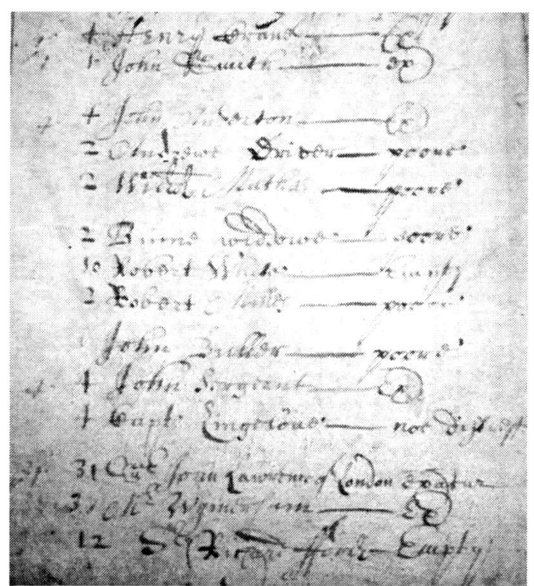

Fig. 3. Extract from the hearth tax list for Putney in 1665, from Henry Crane on the west side of Putney Hill up to Robert White at the bowling green and down the east side of the Hill to Sir John Lawrence at Coalecroft and Dawes Wymondsold and Sir Richard Ford in the High Street (Nos. 130 to 143 in the directory).

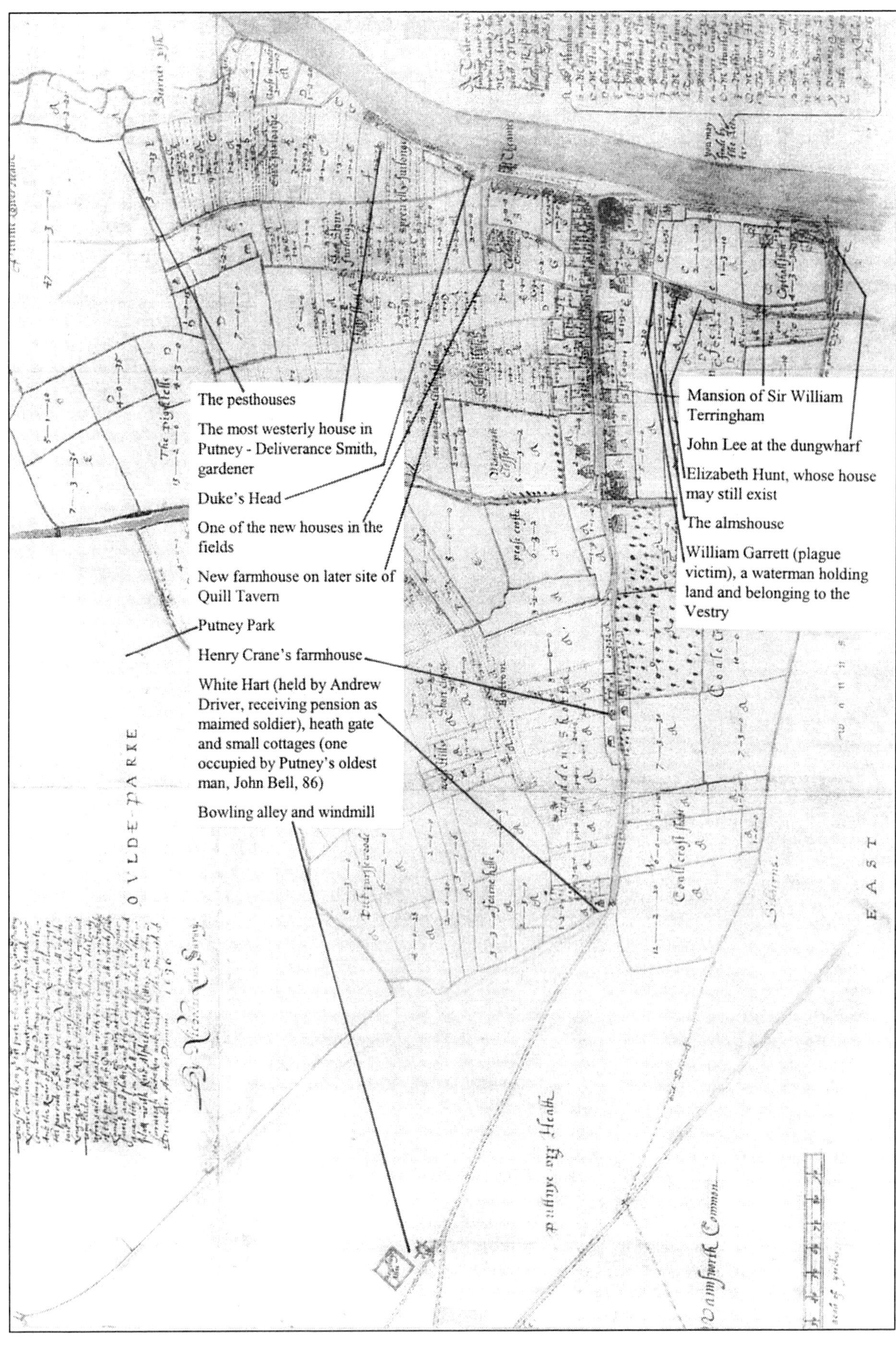

Fig. 4. Places of interest in Putney in 1665, marked on the map of 1636.

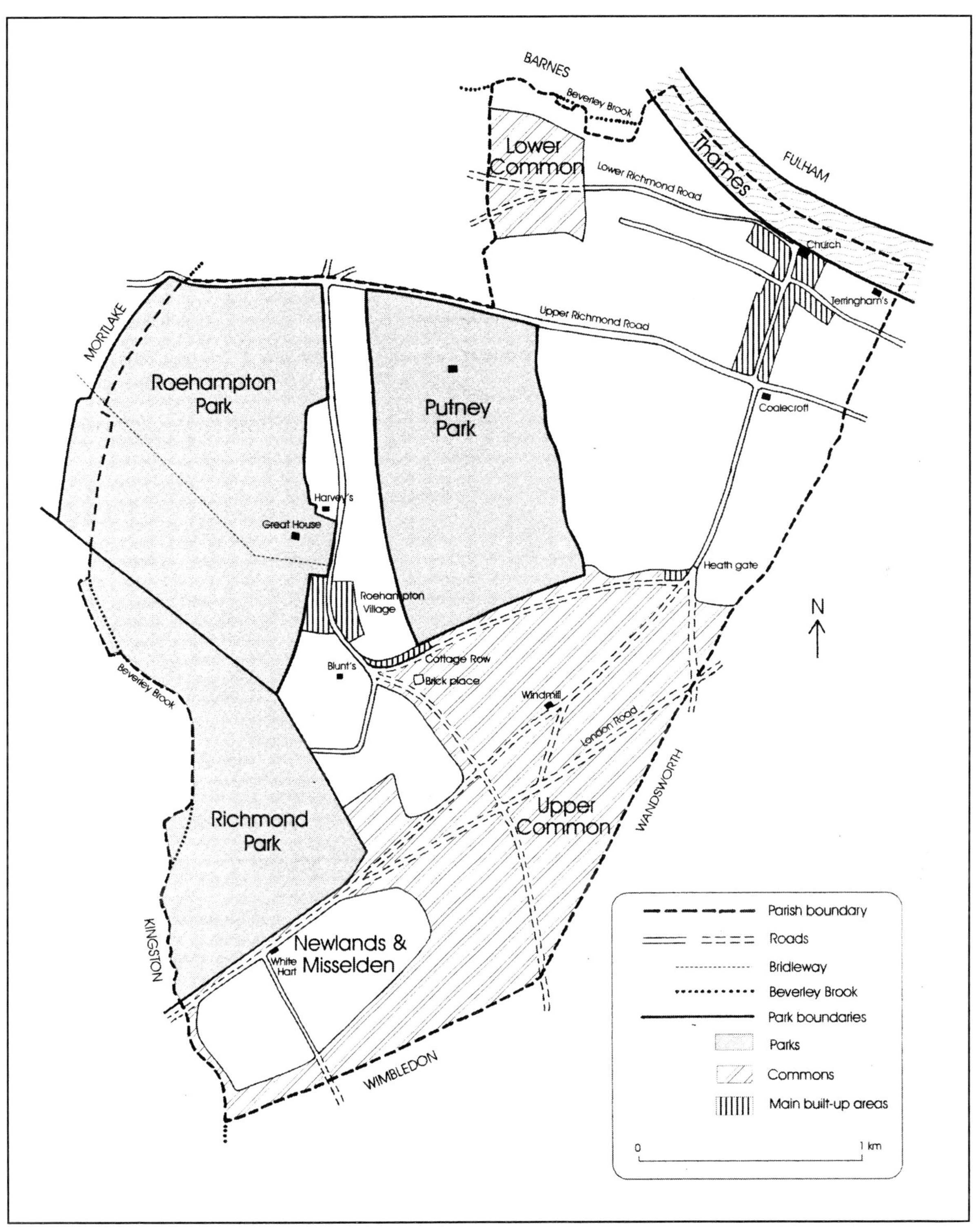

Fig. 5. Reconstruction map of Putney parish in 1665. There was also a small detached area by the Thames in Barnes, consisting of meadow. The boundary with Wandsworth on the Upper Common was disputed; the map shows the boundary agreed in 1787. The built-up areas marked are approximate, especially in Roehampton. Only selected buildings are shown outside those areas. Some of the land in Putney and Roehampton Parks was farmland.

the list also has John Pilkington, described elsewhere as an 'inmate' in the house in 1662. Where, as in this case, dwellings had been subdivided, it must sometimes have been hard to know who was a householder and who a lodger.

However, the court rolls occasionally indicate more dwellings than there are householders in the 1665 list.[5] Also, some individuals known to have been living in Putney are omitted, including some recorded in tax or rate lists of both 1664 and 1668. Most seriously, the 1665 list seems to omit many of the poorest householders: of the 47 householders listed as exempt in Putney in 1664, 19 are left out in 1665. Three or four had died, but many of the others were clearly still alive and in Putney, such as widow Cutt at the heath gate. Similarly in Roehampton, four householders listed as exempt in 1664 are omitted.[6]

Obviously dwellings were sometimes empty, which could explain some discrepancies between list and court rolls, and although Rogers sometimes recorded empty dwellings he may not have done so consistently. There were also sometimes good reasons for people being omitted, such as temporary absence (especially at sea in the case of watermen) or a period as a lodger. Additions to the list (shown in

Fig. 8. Another early nineteenth-century view, from slightly further up the High Street, showing Anne Rogers' buildings with the four gables, and on the right-hand side some of Robert Huntley's buildings. The low building with the arcade, slightly set back, is the one shown in Fig. 19. On the left are what appear to be the two wings of Jane Hubbert's mansion (No. 51), of which otherwise no views are known.

italics in Part II) have therefore been made sparingly. 19 of the exempt poor of 1664 are added (15 in Putney and four in Roehampton).[7] So are nine other householders: for these there is good evidence from 1665 or from both before and after 1665 that they were householders in Putney then.[8] A case could be made for including several others,[9] but no-one for whom there is not strong evidence of being a householder *in 1665* has been added. The 1665 list is therefore not absolutely complete, but with the 28 additions it is likely to cover virtually all of Putney and Roehampton's householders.

Captain Bunn's conversations

An example of the value of knowing where everyone lived is provided by Thomas Bunn, a former sea-captain friendly with Samuel Pepys.[10] Bunn lodged in 1669-71 with Henry Tunstall, glasier, at the lower end of the High Street (No. 184), having been advised by a surgeon to go to the country 'to better ayre'. Anna Knipe, wife of Richard Knipe, who then lived at No. 36 or 37 on the west side of the High Street,[11] became acquainted with him through 'sitting neare ye house of ye said Mr Tunstale and spinning shoemakers thread & [Bunn] often sitting in the porch of ye said Mr Tunstale house and often there discoursing together'. She was therefore able to give evidence that he had intended to leave all his property to Henry Tunstall and his daughter Martha rather than to his relations; he was reported to have said of Martha that 'if he were young enough for her he would marry her before any woeman in the world'.[12] (Martha in fact married a man who became Governor of Tangiers, and then lived for 20 years from 1688 at St George's manor, Long Island, New York.)[13] The High Street was a busy road by seventeenth-century standards, but Bunn and Knipe were apparently able to sit in front of their houses on opposite sides of the street and have a conversation.

2. Putney and Roehampton in 1665

A tour

Peter Rogers began at what was then (as in 1636) the westernmost house in Putney: that of Deliverance Smith, gardener, north of Lower Richmond Road (houses on the east side of Bendemeer Road now occupy the site). East of it were several other houses of gardeners. He proceeded towards what was then Windsor Street (now the eastern part of Lower Richmond Road), where there were a few dwellings on the riverside north of the road, as well as large houses south of it, including one with 18 hearths.

Turning up the west side of the High Street he recorded Putney's main inns opposite the church and the ferry landing (the successor of one of them, then the White Lion but currently the Walkabout, still stands there). Continuing southwards, there was a mixture of large houses and small cottages (most with one or two hearths) as far as the field path from Putney town into the fields (now Felsham Road). Here Rogers diverted westwards to record the scatter of cottages and farmhouses recently built in the fields, including his own. There were not many of these in 1665, but their number was increasing.

Back in the High Street there was an almost unbroken row of small or smallish houses (with from one to six hearths) almost as far as our Chelverton Road, and then three large houses (one recently-built of brick).[1] The High Street itself had been paved at great expense in 1656, before which it was famous for 'deepnes and dangerous mires'.[2] South of Upper Richmond Road were a row of cottages at the foot of the Hill (next to the pound), a farmhouse half-way up the Hill and a clump of cottages at the top of the Hill near the gate which prevented animals straying from the common. Finally Rogers reached the windmill and bowling alley (or green) on the Heath – a popular place of entertainment in summer (Fig. 9); the southern part of Heathview Gardens now occupies the site of the bowling green.[3]

Fig. 9. The windmill and bowling green in 1636.

He next returned down the east side of the Hill, where there were only three dwellings. But at the foot of the Hill was Putney's second-largest house, known as Coalecroft, with 31 hearths and occupied in 1665 by Sir John Lawrence, Lord Mayor of London. Its grounds included virtually the whole of Putney parish east of the Hill.

Rogers now came to the east side of the High Street, which was quite different in character from the west side, being dominated by the large houses of Putney's merchants and gentlemen.

Fig. 10. Park Lodge, Putney Bridge Road, the older part of which (shown here) is almost certainly the four-hearth house occupied by Elizabeth Hunt, widow of a gardener, in 1665 (No. 159). The house has been much added to, notably by a Victorian extension to the east.

First he recorded Dawes Wymondsold's mansion, Putney's largest house, with 37 hearths, on the site now occupied by Putney Station. The house had been built in 1635-6 by Sir Abraham Dawes, Wymondsold's grandfather.[4] Beyond it were four more large houses, the tithe barn, a few smaller houses and then another large house with spacious grounds near the corner of the High Street and Putney Bridge Road (then Wandsworth Lane). Putney's stocks were at that corner.[5]

A few buildings stood south of Putney Bridge Road, including the almshouse and a gardener's house which appears to have survived to the present (Fig. 10). North of the road were a cluster of houses in the north-east corner of the parish near

Fig. 11. St Mary's church, seen from the river. The structure on the left with two tall windows was the vestry house, built in 1629, the centre of local government. To its right are the stairs to the Countess of Devonshire's gallery of 1668. The clock on the tower was installed in 1638.

the dungwharf (at the eastern end of the present Deodar Road), two large houses facing the river (with 17 and 10 hearths), the brewhouse on the eastern side of Brewhouse Lane, and some cottages in Brewhouse Lane. All that then remained were the dwellings east of the High Street between Putney Bridge Road and the church and Church House (with 11 hearths) east of the church. The church itself (St Mary's) was a largely medieval building, of which the tower and some other parts survive today (colour plate 5 and Fig. 11). It was increasingly inadequate for the growing town: a gallery had been constructed in 1625, and others were added from 1654 to 1668.[6]

Around Putney's dwellings were its fields. These had mostly been open fields in 1636, but they appear to have been enclosed in the 1640s or 1650s,[7] making possible the rising number of new dwellings out in the fields. There were probably many more hedges than when Lane drew his map in 1636. The land nearest the river, on fertile gravel soils, was generally occupied by market gardeners; further south there were larger holdings, farmed less intensively. Any trees were in hedges or gardens or on the commons; there were no woods. The upper and lower commons were used for pasturing animals and for obtaining wood, and could have other uses too; Pepys recorded in May 1667 that the king (Charles II) had gone to run horses on Putney Heath.[8]

It was less easy for a tax collector to follow a clear route in Roehampton (see Fig. 54). The collector naturally started with Roehampton Great House (Fig. 12), occupied by Christian, Countess Dowager of Devonshire. With 57 hearths, this was the largest house in Surrey apart from Lambeth Palace.[9] It had its own chapel, large formal gardens to the north and a 350-acre park. Grove House, part of Roehampton University, now occupies the site of the house. Nearby was the Harvey family's mansion, with 20 hearths (its site later passed to the Convent of the Sacred Heart, and is also now part of Roehampton University).

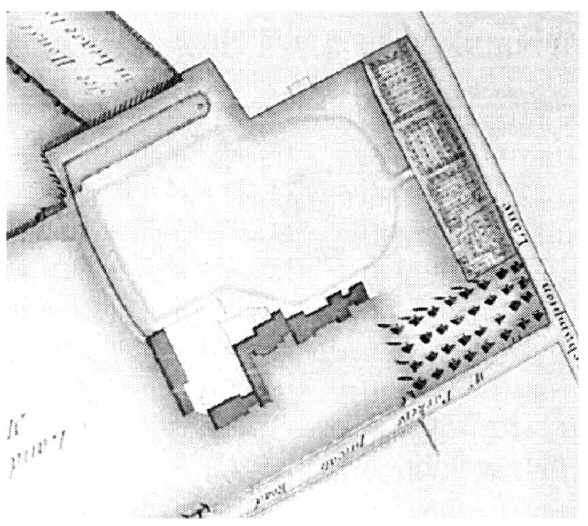

Fig. 12. Roehampton Great House, shown on a plan of about 1780, shortly before it was demolished. Roehampton Lane is to the right; Clarence Lane is at the bottom. No views of the house are known to exist.

Apart from those, Roehampton's larger houses, including its farmhouses and inns, were mostly in and around Roehampton Street (the part of our Roehampton Lane in the Downshire House area). This was the historic centre of Roehampton.[10] But there was also a row of cottages (later known as Cottage Row) along the north side of what is now Roehampton High Street. These had all been built in the previous 70 or so years, on land enclosed from the common, and eventually would come to be regarded as Roehampton village.[11] These were probably the poorest housing in the entire parish, and most had just one hearth. There were a few houses elsewhere, including a large one south of the present village, with ten hearths, and an inn (the White Hart) and a farmhouse on former woodland in Putney Vale. Roehampton's open fields had been enclosed a century earlier, in about 1567.[12]

Neither tax collector listed the large house (12 hearths) which had replaced or been adapted from the old hunting lodge in the medieval Putney Park. The park contained 248 acres and was an oblong area whose bounds were Upper Richmond Road in the north, approximately the line of the present Larpent Avenue in the east, the common in the south and the western edge of the Dover House Estate in the west. It had ceased to be a deer park in 1636, after which parts of it were ploughed, but it remained intact as a separate estate. The house stood within the bend in the present Putney Park Lane.[13]

Households and population

Using the standard method of multiplying the average annual number of baptisms by 30, Putney parish's population in the 1660s was about 1,500. It is possible that this under-states the true number, both because of omissions from the register[14] and because of the high proportion of household servants, who were generally unmarried, so the population may have been somewhat over 1,500.

How consistent is this with the 1665 tax list? With the added names, there were 222 householders in Putney and 64 in Roehampton. Converting this into population figures requires an estimate of the number of people per household. It has been argued that average household size outside London was normally about 4.3 persons,[15] but the figure is likely to have been relatively high in Putney because of the number of large houses occupied by merchants and gentlemen. According to the table of population compiled by the contemporary statistician, Gregory King, the average size of household for knights was 13, for esquires ten and for gentlemen, greater office-holders and greater merchants eight, though recent research suggests that each of these figures should be reduced by about one.[16] There were certainly many more in Roehampton Great House and in Putney's two schools; Henry Portman claimed to have 20 teachers and servants at his school in 1649.[17] King estimated that there were 5.5 persons per household within the walls of the City of London, though in some parishes the figure was much higher.[18] In Putney parish in 1791 there were 5.2 persons per household.[19] Using the 5.2 figure, for want of anything better, the population in 1665 was about 1,500 (1,150 in Putney and 330 in Roehampton), which is consistent with the total obtained by counting baptisms.

On the other hand that was the total with all the dwellings occupied, and some of the large ones were undoubtedly used as summer houses by merchants and gentlemen, who generally had houses in the City or Westminster as well.[20] The population was therefore higher in summer than winter. The 1665 list was made during what was regarded as winter, and 29 dwellings in Putney and ten in Roehampton are listed as empty. This may sometimes have reflected the actual situation, rather than just an attempt to avoid liability for tax.[21] Five of the merchants' houses are listed as empty, and so are three of the inns – the Red Lion, the Bull and the bowling green inn; the latter is later recorded opening for the summer in March or April.[22]

Building and builders

Putney was growing rapidly in 1665, and there were twice as many households as in 1617, just 50 years earlier, when a detailed manorial survey had been made.[23] Many sites in the area already built-up in 1617 had gained two or three additional houses by 1665, and about 67, or 60%, of the extra houses were within that area.[24] But the growth was not evenly spread: 31 of these extra houses were on just six sites: Webb's plot and wharf in Lower Richmond Road (four extra), a Wymondsold plot opposite the church (five extra), Thundering Alley west of the High Street (six extra), a Pettiward plot opposite the parsonage (at least 11 extra) and two adjoining plots in Brewhouse Lane (five extra). On a few sites, mostly east of the High Street, there were *fewer* dwellings than in 1617.

About 44 new houses were outside the former built-up area, where there had been only six dwellings in 1617 (one in Felsham Road, one at the dungwharf, three on the Hill and one at the bowling green). Now there were ten near the riverside from the present Duke's Head westwards, eight in and around Felsham Road, three in or near Upper Richmond Road, eleven on the Hill, two at the bowling green on the heath, and 16 plus the almshouse in Putney Bridge Road or near the dungwharf. Clearly it was now much easier to build in the fields. Deliverance Smith's remained the furthest house westwards, but it was no longer so by 1668.

The new dwellings in 1665 included two mansions on new sites: one on the present site of Chelverton Road, built in the 1640s or 1650s, and one by the river north of Putney Bridge Road.

In general it was land belonging to the smaller landholders which was most heavily developed, perhaps because the trouble of collecting small rents from poor householders was not worth the effort for the larger landholders. For example, Richard Fisher, carpenter, acquired a half-acre strip in Glasinghall Shot in 1664, lying across the church path, now Quill Lane, just east of the present Modder Place. He sold parts of it to another carpenter and a bricklayer (Thomas Denning and Richard Crane) almost immediately, and by 1667 it contained two dwellings – the first in the Quill Lane area; it is not clear whether they were already there in 1665.[25] Pepper Alley, off the High Street just south of Felsham Road, originated in 1646-51 when Thomas Juer, waterman, converted a barn into two tenements and possibly added other dwellings; by 1680 there were seven tenements on the site.[26]

Fig. 13. The Castle public house in Putney Bridge Road in about 1880. The site, which contained four cottages, was acquired by Thomas Kentish, a carpenter, in 1665, and the style of the building suggests that it was constructed by Kentish shortly afterwards.

An exception to the general rule was a plot west of the High Street (Nos. 93-105) belonging to John Pettiward, who was a major landholder. Here Thomas Denning, carpenter, appears to have had an agreement with Pettiward to pay the rent for the entire plot, amounting to £50 a year. The plot already contained ten dwellings in 1658, and in 1663 Denning was prosecuted for building three tenements next to his own (No. 95) without attaching to them the legally-required (but completely impractical) four acres.[27]

One result of the spreading of buildings to new areas was that those farming the land no longer lived in the High Street. The last of the ancient farmhouses in the High Street to be used as such was apparently that of Robert Boughton, almost opposite the parsonage,[28] though the house itself was already subdivided in 1617. Boughton, described in the parish register as 'an ancient farmour', died in 1661, and by 1665 the site contained six dwellings, one of them (No. 87) occupied by Nicholas Meades, carpenter, who had probably built them. In 1665 there were no husbandmen or gardeners living in the High Street except Christopher Miller, gardener (No. 118), and Francis Button, husbandman (No. 120); neither remained there in 1668, and Button had moved westwards to a new dwelling in or close to Upper Richmond Road.[29] In 1665 the husbandmen and gardeners generally lived in houses in or around Putney Hill, Felsham Road, Lower Richmond Road and Putney Bridge Road.

In Roehampton too the number of dwellings had doubled since 1617, from 30 to 64, but there had been a much more complete transformation than in Putney. Both Roehampton Great House and the Harveys' mansion dated from the early 1620s, and the former acquired a 350-acre park, enclosed in 1633, which swallowed up much of Roehampton's farmland.[30] Other farmland was taken in the 1630s for Richmond Park. The grounds of the two mansions had replaced part of Roehampton's main street, but additional houses seem to have been added to that street, and there were new farmhouses and other dwellings south of the present village. Another important development was the growth of Cottage Row, which had just three houses in 1617 but probably about 14 by 1665.

However, the number of houses in Roehampton seems to have peaked in about 1665 and then declined: the number of chargeable houses fell from 49 in 1665 to only 32 in 1674, and that this was not just an accident of recording is indicated by the fact that the *total* number of houses in 1713 was only 42.[31] What was happening is unclear, but cottages may well have been demolished to improve the surroundings of the large houses, and eventually to build new large houses.

Putney parish in context

The fact that hearth tax records survive for most of England means that the social standing of Putney and Roehampton can be compared with the rest of the country, as well as with neighbouring parishes. It has been argued that the best form of comparison is on the basis of the proportion of dwellings with three or more hearths.[32] That proportion was 42% in Putney, 30% in Roehampton and 39% in the parish as a whole.[33] The overall figure was slightly higher than in Surrey as a whole (36%), and Surrey itself had the highest proportion of any county except Middlesex (46%). In fact the proportion tended to be higher the closer to London, and the figure for Putney alone is comparable to that for the other Thames-side parishes of north-east Surrey (44%).[34] Putney was clearly a prosperous parish in a prosperous area.

As regards very large houses, Putney parish was distinctive even in the London area. It had 25 houses with ten or more hearths, a number exceeded among parishes within 17 miles of London only by Chelsea (29), Fulham (27), Greenwich (52), Hammersmith (27), Isleworth (35), Kingston (28), Richmond (33) and Romford with Havering (32).[35] As for the largest houses, with 20 or more hearths, Putney parish had five, matched by Greenwich, Richmond and Romford with Havering and exceeded only by Chelsea (six), Isleworth (seven) and Chiswick (eight).

At the other end of the social scale, comparisons of the proportion of exempt households are rendered hazardous by variations in recording. Putney parish's proportion in 1664 was 24% (24% in Putney, 26% in Roehampton). This was about average for north-east Surrey (28%), but less than in Surrey as a whole (34%). The figures for Surrey and its north-east part were low but not exceptional, since several English counties had lower proportions.[36] Within the local area, Putney parish's 24% was lower than in Wandsworth and Battersea (42% and 36%), but higher than in Wimbledon, Barnes and Mortlake (14%, 10% and 18%) and similar to Richmond and Clapham (26% and 21%).[37] How much reliance can be placed on these figures is uncertain, but it is clear that being a prosperous parish did not necessarily mean that Putney had a smaller proportion of poor families than other places.

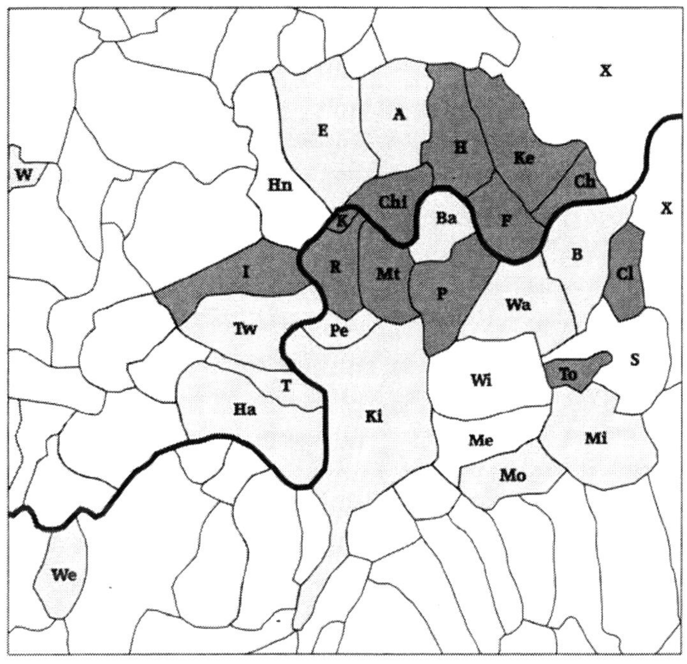

Fig. 14. Parishes west of London, showing the number of houses with ten or more hearths per thousand acres in about 1673. Few parishes other than Thames-side ones had large numbers of such houses. Key: dark grey, 11 or more (Putney 11.9); light grey, 3.5 to 8; white, 0 to 2.5 (except where marked X). Places: A Acton, B Battersea, Ba Barnes, Ch Chelsea, Chi Chiswick, Cl Clapham, E Ealing, F Fulham, H Hammersmith, Ha Hampton, Hn Hanwell, I Isleworth, K Kew, Ke Kensington, Ki Kingston, Me Merton, Mi Mitcham, Mo Morden, Mt Mortlake, P Putney, Pe Petersham, R Richmond, S Streatham, T Teddington, To Tooting, Tw Twickenham, W West Drayton, Wa Wandsworth, We Weybridge, Wi Wimbledon, X not covered.

3. The people

The rich

In 1657 it was said that the Minister of Putney might have a considerable influence on the City of London 'by reason of the quality of the cittizens of greate worth and value in the said towne', and in 1667, on a visit to Putney, Pepys 'stepped into church to look upon the fine people there, whereof there is great store'.[1]

The voluntary subscription made in July 1665 to meet the costs of plague nicely grades the well-to-do in Putney.[2] Heading the list, at £3 each, were Sir John Lawrence and Dawes Wymondsold esquire. Wymondsold was the most substantial landholder in Putney by a long way, and, as indicated above, lived in Putney's largest house, with 37 hearths, at the top of the High Street. His two grandfathers, Sir Abraham Dawes, a merchant and farmer of the customs (d.1640), and William Wymondsold, an official of the Exchequer (d.1664), had come to Putney together in about 1619 and at first lived in the same house, but quarrelled irretrievably over possession of Dawes' mansion and some of his land in the late 1630s. Since then the Dawes family had been penalised as having profited under Charles I and had lost much of their land, while William Wymondsold had been able to add greatly to his estate.[3] Sir John Lawrence (colour plate 1), in the second largest house – 31 hearths – and holder of all Putney's land east of the Hill, was Lord Mayor of London in 1665 and leader of the City's anti-court faction. He had an income of £2000 a year in 1660.[4]

Fig. 15. Monument in Putney church to Daniel Belt (c.1616-1697), who occupied a house east of the brewhouse in 1665 (No. 177) and shortly afterwards moved to Church House (No. 196).

In the next rank, paying £2 each, were John Pettiward (colour plate 4) and three knights. Their houses had 20, 16, 12 and 11 hearths respectively. Pettiward, a merchant and London Alderman, was another substantial landholder in Putney; he had inherited the land in 1658 from his father-in-law, Henry White, a baker and moneylender of Putney.[5] The three knights were Sir

Thomas Chamberlayne, Sir Francis Clarke and Sir Richard Ford, all merchants and the latter two Aldermen (Ford was Lord Mayor in 1670). Chamberlayne had been a major in the parliamentary army; he married a daughter of Philip Burlamachi, Charles I's financier, who had occupied the same house in Putney.[6]

Eight merchants or gentlemen paid £1.10s.0d. or £1; their hearths ranged from nine to 14. The five who paid just 10s. were a gentleman with a relatively small house (Daniel Belt with ten hearths; Fig. 15), a musician (John Hingeston; Fig. 16), two schoolmasters (Henry Portman and Noah Bridges) and the Minister of Putney (Edward Sclater). Their hearths ranged from six to ten, apart from Portman's 18. Sclater, who became Minister of Putney in 1663, had strong Royalist views, and was later, under James II, to declare himself a Roman Catholic.[7] Hingeston was a court musician; he had been organist to Oliver Cromwell, later served Charles II, and left money in his will to 'my ffellow servants of his Majesties private musique and Gentlemen of his Chappell'.[8] Bridges (Fig. 17) was a mathematician and had been Clerk of the Parliament which sat at Oxford in 1643-4; his school probably existed from 1647 until his death in 1672, and Portman's from 1638 or earlier possibly until 1702.[9] Among the women with large houses, Mrs Hubbert was the widow of the lord of Allfarthing manor in Wandsworth.

Although the merchants and gentlemen generally had nine or more hearths, some had fewer. John

Fig. 16. Portrait of John Hingeston (c.1606-1683), court musician under Oliver Cromwell and Charles II (No. 54). He described Orlando Gibbons in his will as 'my ever honoured master', and he was godfather to Henry Purcell.

Fig. 17. Noah Bridges (c.1613-1672), who ran a school for boys at Putney, shown in a miniature by Samuel Cooper.

Oughton and Robert Lewis, gentlemen and neighbours at the lower end of the High Street, each had only six hearths, and William Ridges, a former Alderman, had just four (despite great wealth).[10] Including these, about 27 householders (13% of the total)[11] fall into the 'rich' category.

Apart from Wymondsold, Lawrence and Pettiward, Putney's merchants and gentlemen held little if any land in Putney. Only three others – Hubbert, Chamberlayne and Terringham – held even the houses they occupied, and in fact Putney's land was rarely on the market (Appendix 1). Most simply leased a house, which provided a convenient retreat a short ferry, horse or coach ride from London for the summer or weekends or whenever time was available – as Defoe later put it, they left the 'sin and seacoal in the busy city' to enjoy the 'gay excursions' of summer.[12] In winter many of the large houses were empty. Merchants and

Fig. 18. Church House, east of the church (No. 196). It had 11 hearths in 1665. There was a great house here by the early sixteenth century. From 1638 or earlier until about 1664 it was occupied by Henry Portman's school, but Portman then moved to a larger house in Lower Richmond Road.

Fig. 19. A house on the east side of the High Street, half-way between the church and Putney Bridge Road, which was clearly standing in 1665 (seen here in about 1893). It was on Huntley land in 1665, and was either the six-hearth house of Robert Lewis, gentleman, or the five-hearth house of Henry Tunstall, glasier (Nos. 183-4).

gentlemen had their own coaches and horses, such as Roger Pettiward's two coach horses and a 'charriot' in 1675,[13] though they also travelled on the river. Transport was not yet good enough for commuting to London.

The inhabitants of the largest houses dominated Putney in every way: they employed many of the people directly, provided custom for tradesmen and watermen, held most of the land and dwellings and filled the office of churchwarden and the Vestry, which handled parish affairs including poor relief. No-one had paid the fine of £10 to avoid having to undertake parish offices such as churchwarden since 1638, though William Harvey of Roehampton was to do so in 1668.[14] The 21 houses with nine or more hearths are likely to have contained about a fifth of Putney's population.[15]

The comfortable

At the next level were householders in reasonably comfortable circumstances, including those with from three to six hearths and many of those with two hearths. They were mostly tradesmen, master craftsmen, husbandmen or gardeners, together with some watermen and the better-off widows. A handful of them became Vestry members and churchwarden. The Vestry in 1665 included the three major innkeepers, Weller, Kite and Rogers, together with Thomas Denning, carpenter (and builder), Walter Sisam, gardener, and Henry Tunstall, glasier, the latter three having two, four and five hearths respectively. Of these only Denning and Sisam held a little land – one rood and two tenements respectively, recently acquired in both cases. There were a few other small landholders not on the Vestry, such as William Garrett, waterman, and Thomas Kentish, carpenter.

Sometimes the source of their prosperity is unknown, and no doubt there was sometimes inherited wealth, as in the case of Edward Juer (two hearths), who lived not only by his earnings as a waterman but on £20 a year left him by his father.[16] A good route to advancement was property development, as shown by Thomas Denning, who by the time of his death in 1703 held 12 leasehold houses in London as well as land in Putney and Barnes.[17] Other carpenters and builders also prospered. But most of Putney's comfortable households are likely to have been sustained just by a solid business such as a smithy, bakery or garden plot. Among the watermen, the better-off, such as Richard Foster with his six hearths, were probably those who had their own boat. For the watermen in particular, the degree of comfort must often have been limited and precarious, especially with advancing age.

The comfortable householders tended to fill offices such as overseer of the poor, and this formed one of the main dividing lines within Putney, between those who participated occasionally in parish life by holding one of the local offices and those who did not. Another sign of status was purchase of the right to a seat in the parish church (usually for a one-off payment of 2s.6d. per seat), though only from

Fig. 20. The interior of St Mary's church, Putney, looking from the chancel towards the west end before the rebuilding in 1836. The gallery across the west end was built in 1625; the others were added between 1654 and 1668. The gallery occupying the furthest arch on the left was built in 1654 by Henry Portman, and his successors at the school continued to use it until 1702.

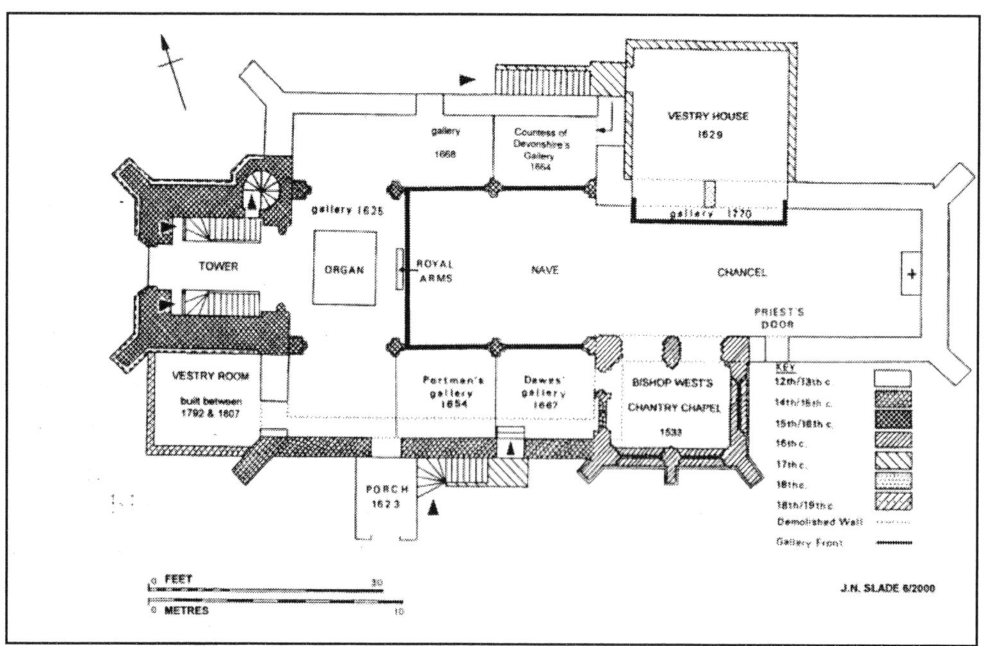

Fig. 21. Plan of St Mary's church before 1836, drawn by Jim Slade. Note the vestry house of 1629, Bishop West's chantry chapel and the galleries. Before the new gallery was built in 1668 only the richer inhabitants paid for reserved seats; after that most of the 'comfortable' and even some poorer inhabitants did so too. Many of the comfortable were accommodated in the front two rows of the galleries of 1625 and 1668. But the most coveted seats, or pews, were those in the nave near the pulpit. For example, Henry Portman's gallery was 'for the seating of his family' (which would have included his pupils), whereas he himself sat in solitary splendour next to the pulpit; the Countess of Devonshire's gallery (authorised 1664 but built 1668) was for her servants, and she also acquired two pews at the junction of nave and chancel. Husbands and wives normally sat separately, however wealthy; so did their children. There was a pew for 'menes daughters', a pew in a gallery for maidservants and benches at the base of the tower for boys.

1668 when a new gallery was built and a higher proportion of pews began to be paid for. Most of the better-off householders purchased seats for themselves and their wives, including a number of watermen, whereas few of the poorer inhabitants did so.[18] Prosperity was also displayed by means of larger or more comfortable houses, quantity and quality of furniture, clothing and employment of domestic servants, such as the maidservant of Thomas Garrett, waterman, in 1671.[19] The value of household goods in inventories correlates reasonably well with the number of hearths.[20] There is little sign in inventories (except those for the great houses) of the consumer goods which were so important later, but Susan Poole of Roehampton had a looking glass and 'hangings' in 1674, Edward King two chests of drawers in 1676 and Richard Fisher a looking glass and window curtains in 1678.[21] An impressionistic count, based on number of hearths, holding of local offices (except that of aleconner, discussed later) and payment for pews, suggests that about 87 householders fell into the relatively comfortable class – 41% of the total.

Table 1. Social composition of Putney and Roehampton's households (%), 1665

	Putney: all householders	*Putney: female householders*	*Roehampton: all householders*	*Roehampton: female householders*
Rich	13	12	5	7
Comfortable	41	24	44	40
Poor, but ratepayers	20	12	20	7
Poor, non-ratepaying, of which:	25	53	31	47
Receiving poor relief	11	35	13	27

Note: Figures for Putney are based on 210 of the 222 dwellings, excluding Nos. 23, 47, 53, 101, 107-8, 116, 129, 158, 185 and 196-7 (mainly those where the landholder appears to be listed). Those for Roehampton are based on 61 of the 64 dwellings, excluding Nos. 220, 239 and 257. Figures may not add up to 100% due to rounding.

The poor

The hearth tax list does not clearly indicate the division between the comfortable and the poorer households – the remaining 46% – because either might have two-hearth houses (which accounted for almost half of all houses), but the division is often apparent from other sources. Many of the poorer householders were not described as poor, and were not exempt from the tax, but did not fill parish offices (except aleconner) or pay for a pew; they perhaps made a tolerable living until they became sick or old, or in the case of watermen were seized by the press gang for service in the navy, leaving their families unprovided for. Almost half of them were watermen.

This is a broadly-drawn category of poorer households. It can be broken down into three smaller categories: those who paid rates (who would not at the time have been regarded as poor), those who neither paid rates nor received poor relief, and those who received poor relief (and within the latter category those who received pensions). The second and third of these categories will be regarded here as the poorest householders.

These poorest householders should have been those exempted from the hearth tax, and should therefore be clearly listed and clearly defined, but in fact are neither of these. Unfortunately Peter Rogers' designations as 'poore' cannot be taken seriously, since they cover many of the comfortable. 47 of the 85 described by Rogers as poor were charged for the hearth tax in 1664 or rates in 1668 or both of these, and even the remaining 38 included Thomas Kentish, a landholder. Also, Rogers simply omitted many of the genuinely exempt.

As for the criteria, the statute set out two reasons for exemption: the property was worth less than £1 per year, and the householder did not pay rates and local taxes 'by reason of his poverty or the smallness of his estate'.[22] The first exemption cannot ever have applied in Putney parish, since even a single room for a pauper or a one-hearth cottage in Roehampton's Cottage Row cost more than £1 a year.[23] Therefore the judgment made about poverty when levying rates should have applied to the hearth tax as well. However, exactly how that judgment was made is unknown. Exemption clearly extended beyond those eligible for poor relief.

For present purposes, the poorest householders are taken to be the 39 listed as exempt in 1664,[24] together with the 14 of those listed as poor by Rogers who did not pay either the 1664 tax or the 1668 rate or who received poor relief in or about 1665,[25] making a total of 53, or about 25% of households. This compares with 24% exempted in 1664, and perhaps 28% in 1668.[26] These figures are somewhat artificial, since the poor did not always form separate households. In particular, the parish tended to place paupers in a single room as lodgers in someone else's house. Also the almshouse could be regarded as 12 separate one-person households, including some of the poorest. Nevertheless, the figures provide a rough guide for distinguishing the poorer ratepaying households (about 20% of households) from the poorest (about 25%).

Among the poorest 53, the largest groups were the 13 watermen and the 18 widows – seven of them widows of watermen. Four were in the clothing trades, which required relatively little skill or capital and so were easy to enter and poorly paid. One was the parish clerk, Christopher Rogers, who held that post for 61 years. Three were described as labourers, but probably others also fell into the labouring category, such as the two gardeners and two husbandmen and at least some of the six for whom no occupation has been identified. 53% of all the households headed by women were among the poorest. Many of the poorest householders appear to have been old, notably John Bell, labourer (No. 132A), who was about 86, and did not die until 1676, aged 97. He had been born in Putney in about 1579, and had seen a remarkable transformation in the parish in that period.

One of the causes of poverty was the press gang, which forcibly recruited men into the Navy. England was at war with the Dutch in 1665, and two Putney householders, Simon Mowden and Thomas Howell junior, both watermen, were at sea, leaving their families to depend on poor relief. A remarkable document from 1672, when England was again at war with the Dutch, illustrates the impact the press gang could have. It is headed 'An account of the poor watermen, of Putney, whose wifes by reson their husbands are gon to sea, and others that are prst, to goe at an howers warning, are not able to pay his Majestys duty of Chimney Money, nor to subsist of themselves without the help of others'. 14 Putney watermen had been pressed, four of them with their servants, and so had the servants of two widows of watermen. Another four watermen had gone to sea, but are carefully distinguished from those pressed. The pressed watermen included some of the poorest householders, including Simon Mowden again (with his servant) and some categorised here as comfortable, such as Richard Penn. The impact on wives and families of the sudden removal of husbands and fathers and the scenes during the 'howers warning' can only be imagined.[27]

The dwellings of the poorest 53 were scattered about, often just where we would expect them, such as two in Thundering Alley (Fig. 22) and one or two in Pepper Alley. The largest clusters were the six or more in Thomas Denning's plot west of the High Street, five at the heath gate and five in Brewhouse Lane.

24 of the 53 poorest (about 11% of all households) received poor relief in or around 1665. Half of these households were headed by women, and two-thirds of those receiving casual poor relief in 1665-6 (not all of whom were householders) were women. Those receiving casual poor relief out of collections made at communion services are listed in full in 1665/6,[28] and included several who also received pensions, but there may have been a few others who received pensions but not casual relief, and so are not recorded as recipients of poor relief. Also, there was a fund established in 1655 and run by the watermen themselves (known as the watermen's chest), using the proceeds of a ferry operated for foot passengers on Sundays, and, although this did not prevent watermen also receiving relief from the parish,[29] there may have been a household or two relieved by the chest but not by the parish. Even taking this into account, only about half of the poorest households received any poor relief from the parish at all, and even in most of these cases the relief was no more than one or two 5s. payments in the year.

Fig. 22. An alley of six extraordinary houses, near the bottom of the High Street on what is now the south side of Weimar Street, known in the eighteenth century as Thundering Alley (Nos. 44-50). Their occupants in 1665 were a basketmaker, five watermen and one whose occupation is unidentified; two of the watermen apparently shared a subdivided house. Each had two hearths (one each in the subdivided house), and the four chimney pots in each stack confirm this number.

William Young, the basketmaker, was exempt from the hearth tax, and the family of one of the watermen was receiving poor relief (the waterman himself being at sea), but another, John Carpenter, held several local offices and was later described as 'one of the most substantiall watermen'. Plague struck four of the seven households in 1665-6, claiming 14 lives, and in the case of the subdivided dwellings probably spread from one to the other.

There had been just a single cottage on the site belonging to Sir Abraham Dawes in 1636, but by 1668 there were six dwellings belonging to Hugh Hubbert. The transfer from the Dawes family to Hubbert was almost certainly in or about 1649, when Hubbert also acquired Allfarthing manor in Wandsworth from Dawes' son, Sir Thomas. In Allfarthing manor Hubbert was an active manager, spending over £700 on new buildings in the 1650s, and Thundering Alley was almost certainly built by Hubbert in the 1650s.

The fact that the dwellings adjoined the garden of Hubbert's own house (No. 51) helps to explain their form. The site was a long narrow one; there was at first a wall or fence on the edge of the plot about nine feet from the chimney breasts (gone by the time of the photo).

Placing the access on the south side (the far side in the photo) would have exposed Hubbert's garden to the noise of the alley, and having the chimneys on the south side would have been unsightly. Windows on the south side were ruled out for similar reasons, and the need for light meant that each floor had to have a single room, about 19 feet by 13 feet, so the chimneys could not be in the middle between rooms. Placing them in the party walls would perhaps have reduced the space too much to allow six dwellings. Therefore both access and chimneys were on the north side, probably enabling Hubbert's garden to be faced by a blank wall, but leaving room only for a single window to light each room. The windows indicate that there was a winding stair in the curved projection and the outer part of the chimneybreast. There appear to have been garretts. In the subdivided house, the ground-floor window was probably replaced by a door giving access to the staircase. The photograph suggests that the alley was never paved; there was just an area of paving around the front doors. Thundering Alley was demolished in the 1880s.

Thus most of these households supported themselves, however inadequately, with little or no help from the parish. In this, Putney was typical of parishes in general.[30] Two of the poorest even managed to pay for pews in the church – Nicholas King, carpenter, and Sarah Randoll, widow of a waterman (P7 and P8). No doubt the poor assisted each other where possible, as indicated by the will of Margery Jones (P4), who left everything she had 'to them tooke paines with her in her sicknesse the neibours that live neare her'.[31]

The poorest of all, unable to support themselves, were those who received pensions from the parish. At least eight householders listed in 1665 received pensions then or later (all but two of whom are also recorded receiving casual poor relief).[32] Four were widows and two were clearly very old. Judging by the level of the poor rate, there cannot have been more than a dozen pensioners at most in 1665.[33] Again, these small numbers were typical.[34]

For two of the poorest 53 householders inventories survive. One exists because when Mary Silley (No. 75) died of plague in 1665 the parish sold her goods to raise money to support her two surviving children.[35] The goods were worth £2.17s.2d., and included two tables, two stools, four chairs, two beds with bedsteads and curtains, one chest, two pairs of sheets, a brass candlestick, 12 napkins, two iron pots, a skillet, a pair of pot hooks, a frying pan, a tin pan, two kettles, old pewter and iron, fire irons, a pair of breeches and a hat. The most valuable item was the pewter (10s.). She also, rather surprisingly, had £2 in cash; perhaps some of her goods had been sold to try and prevent the parish getting them. As she had died of plague her own clothing was probably regarded as worthless. The parish apprenticed her boy to Robert Combes, waterman, and her girl to Goodwife Kite, innholder's wife.

The probate inventory of William Young of Thundering Alley (No. 44), another plague victim, lists goods worth £6.18s.11d. These included kitchen equipment such as two spits and fire irons, but no furniture in what appears to have been the downstairs room except a little table, a round table and a cupboard. Probably upstairs were the bed and bolster, two bedsteads, bedclothes, clothes and trunk.

Fig. 23. The almshouse in Putney Bridge Road, built by Sir Abraham Dawes in the 1630s (No. 158). Its successor, of 1861, still occupies the site.

There were 10 bushels of coal. A 'bodkin thimble ring' and 'silver hooke' were probably connected with Young's trade. The only items worth more than 6s. were the pewter (£1.10s.0d.), the round table (8s.) and the bed and bolster and furnishings (17s.).[36] The most surprising item is the round table, which was a fashionable item, rare before the mid-seventeenth century. Young was perhaps on the borderline of exemption from the hearth tax. The proportions of different types of goods for Silley and Young respectively were beds and bed-linen 32 and 33, eating utensils 18 and 25, furniture 21 and 16, kitchen equipment 18 and 11, clothing 5 and 7, trade goods 0 and 5 and table linen 5 and 2.

The almshouse in Putney Bridge Road (Fig. 23) had been founded by Sir Abraham Dawes by 1636, for 'twelve poor indigent, decayed and decreped almsmen and almeswomen'. Each occupant had one room and a garden, and there was a pump yard at the west end.[37] In 1665 it accommodated three men and nine women. The accounts, kept by John Dawes, indicate that the occupants provided their own furniture, but received 'quartridge' usually of 15s. or 16s. every three months (just over 1s. per week).[38] Many of the householders of 1665 ended their days there, namely Peter Rogers, Thomas Miller, Elizabeth Duffin, John Smith, John Costrell, Thomas Howell, Robert White, Frances Harwood, Alexander Baker, Edward Miller, widow Haughton, widow Bosman, Mrs Mary Norman, Lewis Ashfield, Edward Juer and, from Roehampton, widow Phillips. Only five of these had been among Putney's poorest 53, and there was only widow Phillips from Roehampton's poorest; of these, four had one hearth in 1665 and two had two. Among the others, one had one hearth, two (Frances Harwood and widow Haughton) had three and all the others two. Four were among those defined here as comfortable, notably Mary Norman, a landholder.

Roehampton

Roehampton was dominated by the Countess of Devonshire's Great House. The Countess (Fig. 24) had occupied it since 1648, making it a centre of royalist intrigue during the Interregnum. The atmosphere of life in the Great House is captured in the following description by a Florentine courtier who visited in 1667:

> She lives in a magnificent palace, behaving as something rather grander than a great princess. ... She is waited on by gentlemen, and dines sumptuously every day. Her house is

> always full of visitors. Her chambers are full of precious furniture and silver. She sits up in a bed of ease ... under a sort of baldacchino. ... The Countess does not move, and only gets up when supported on the arms of two extremely beautiful damsels. Her 86 years of age [actually 72] and the paralytic disease she has in her neck, which makes her head constantly turn from side to side like clockwork, do not prevent her from wearing petticoats of pearly cloth embroidered with flowers in bright colours, with large quantities of lace-work in silver thread.[39]

In June 1660 Stephen Charlton wrote that 'The King and the two Dukes dined upon Saturday last at Roehampton, at the Countess of Devonshire's, and General Monk with them, where they were gallantly treated, and after dinner the King and the two Dukes danced with the ladies above an hour, and danced rarely well.'[40] The Countess's biographer noted that the King with other members of the royal family often dined with her, 'and [would] sometimes break in upon her on a sudden after hunting'. By the King and others she was 'reputed to live greater than any subject whatsoever, as to hospitality, resort and retinue'.[41]

The Countess clearly needed numerous staff, and many of them were named in her will of 1673. They included her 'first waytinge gentlewoman', 'second waytinge gentlewoman', 12 other women prefixed 'Mrs' (perhaps her 'gentlewomen'), a stillhouse woman, three chambermaids, two laundry-maids, two house-maids, 'an old servant', a dairy maid, two other women, a bailiff, a carter, a household chaplain, an organist, a steward, the 'gentleman of my horse', a servant described as a gentleman, seven other men (all 'Mr') who may have been servants, the groom of the chambers, the housekeeper, the clerk of the kitchen, the head

Fig. 24. Detail from the portrait of Christian, Dowager Countess of Devonshire (1595-1675) by Daniel Mytens. The Countess occupied Roehampton Great House from 1648 until her death, purchasing it in 1650. It was later occupied by her son and then his widow until her death in 1689.

butler, the under-butler, the master cook, the second, third and fourth cooks, two kitchen boys, a coachman, a postillion, a stable-groom, the porter of the hall, the first footman, two other footmen, a porter, a head gardener, a second gardener and an under-gardener – a possible total of 61 servants.[42] Of course most of these would have moved when the Countess did, leaving only a few such as the bailiff and the gardeners at Roehampton, and only from 1666 did she live permanently at Roehampton, letting out her London house. None of those named in her will appears in the 1665 list, as they did not have their own separate households, but coachmen often lived out, and Thomas Butler (No. 221), with two hearths in 1665, described himself in his will of 1672 as the Countess's coachman.[43]

William Harvey, with 20 hearths, will also have had numerous servants, but nothing like as many as the Countess. He had succeeded his father (colour plate 7), a merchant, there in 1661, and was a nephew of the William Harvey who discovered the circulation of the blood and who spent his last years at Roehampton (dying there in 1657).[44] The third substantial house, with ten hearths, had been occupied by Captain John Blunt, but was empty in 1665. The old main street and the area south of the present village were dominated by husbandmen and a few substantial tradesmen such as a baker, an innholder and a farrier. About 15 of these filled virtually all the local offices in turn. One of them, Nicholas Waxham, was a member of Putney Vestry, as was Thomas Nuthall, gentleman and estate steward. There were few really poor householders in the old main street.

But on the edge of the common, on what is now the northern side of Roehampton High Street, was a concentration of poverty unmatched anywhere else in the parish. Among its 14 or so cottages were 11 with only one hearth, and there were 11 householders who fell into the poorest category, including five who at some stage received poor relief.[45] In total, Roehampton had about 19 householders comparable to the poorest 53 in Putney – a somewhat higher proportion of all householders than in Putney.[46] They included seven widows, two labourers and three described as husbandmen. They may have benefited more than Putney's poor from private charity, as the Countess of Devonshire was reputed to be bountiful to the poor, distributing money through her chaplain.[47] The proportions of Roehampton's householders regarded here as comfortable and as poor but able to pay rates were similar to those in Putney.[48]

The inhabitants of the Newlands area (now Putney Vale), including John Hulke, innkeeper at the White Hart from the 1650s to 1687,[49] seem to have taken no part in Roehampton life. Hulke never held any local office, and two of his children were baptised in Kingston.[50]

John Farmer and Nicholas Gladwyn were the only Roehampton inhabitants who paid for pews in Putney church, which suggests a certain detachment from Putney among Roehampton people. Whether Roehampton people were already making use of the chapel at the Great House, as they did later, is not known. It was certainly very difficult to persuade them to pay the rate for repair of Putney's church in 1668,[51] and Putney's removal in 1669 of Roehampton's ancient right to elect its own churchwarden was perhaps in retaliation for this. Roehampton was also notable for its small group of Quakers in the late 1660s and 1670s.

A stable community?

People moved from parish to parish in past centuries much more than is sometimes realised, and this applied at Putney too. 33 of the 197 householders listed on Lady Day 1664 were not listed again a year later, although in many cases there is an obvious reason, such as death, or moving to the almshouse or becoming a lodger.[52] Of the 157 reasonably well-off householders in 1665 (i.e. all except the 53 poorest),[53] about 84 – just over half – were listed again as hearth tax payers in 1674, and this seems to have been a typical proportion after a decade or so in seventeenth-century England.[54] For some, especially the more prosperous, there were strong reasons for remaining where they were, such as a business or a lease. On the other hand many, such as Jonathan Whitehorne (No. 2), formerly of Mortlake and probably a labourer, were no more than a transient presence in Putney. If we could extend the analysis beyond householders to include servants, apprentices and children we would undoubtedly find a much more rapid turnover of population.

Fig. 25. View in Lower Richmond Road eastwards towards the church in 1823. The gables on the right are those of Clyde House (see Figs. 38 and 39). The brick building on the left with two windows in the gable-end may be Margaret Haughton's three-hearth house which was under construction in 1665 (No. 26).

4. Earning a living

Using the parish register, quarter sessions records and other sources, it is possible to identify the occupations of the great majority of Putney's householders. The frailty of occupational data has often been emphasised: people might change occupations and might carry on several occupations at once. But what is sought here is not so much precise statistics as a general view of how Putney's people supported themselves and why Putney was growing.

Some householders (about 22 in total) made their money away from Putney, usually in London. This applies to most of those with nine hearths or more, except the two schoolmasters, three innholders, the bowling green manager and the brewer, and to some of those with fewer than nine. Nine of the largest houses were occupied by merchants.

Men's work

Table 2 sets out the occupations of male householders earning their livings in Putney.

Table 2. Occupations of male householders earning their livings in Putney in 1665.

Category	No.	%	Number in each occupation
River transport	54	40	51 watermen, 1 bargeman, 1 wharfinger, 1 ship carpenter
Agriculture	23	17	11 gardeners, 9 husbandmen, 3 labourers
Food & drink	24	18	9 victuallers, 3 innholders, 4 poulterers, 3 butchers, 2 bakers, 2 brewers, 1 brewer's servant
Building	11	8	7 carpenters, 2 bricklayers, 1 glasier, 1 locksmith
Clothing	7	5	3 tailors, 3 shoemakers, 1 dyer
Road transport	4	3	1 coachman, 1 farrier, 1 drayman, 1 wheelwright
Misc. trade	7	5	2 coopers, 2 chandlers, 1 blacksmith, 1 tallow chandler, 1 basketmaker
Professional	5	4	2 schoolmasters, 1 clergyman, 1 parish clerk, 1 barber surgeon
	135	100	

Note: Judgments have been made where more than one occupation is recorded: six of those listed here were also victuallers; two watermen, a gardener and a husbandman were also described as labourers. The categories are also somewhat arbitrary, e.g. farriers and blacksmiths might also assist those engaged in agriculture. Four women continuing their husbands' trades are included.

The proportion of watermen is particularly striking, and greatly exceeded that at Wandsworth and Richmond – about 14% and 16% respectively.[1] The watermen conveyed goods and passengers up and down the river as well as operating the cross-river ferry between Putney and Fulham. Some may have traded in goods brought from London, which would explain the six hundredweight of cheese in the house of William Cooke, waterman, in 1662,[2] and they probably also obtained goods in London at the request of Putney people. The land by the river east of the present Duke's Head public house, previously common land, was leased to the watermen of Putney in 1666 'to land and fasten their boats on'.[3] Fishermen are rarely recorded at Putney.

Fig. 26a & b. Halfpenny token issued in 1668 by Richard Broughton, waterman (No. 188), showing the arms of the Watermen's Company.

The rarity of labourers at Putney is puzzling – at most 5%,[4] compared with 23%

Fig. 27a & b. Typical Thames craft, taken from a view of Lambeth Palace in 1697. They include a ferry carrying a coach and horses, similar to the one which operated between Putney and Fulham.

at Wandsworth and 16% at Richmond. Probably many of those for whom no occupation is recorded were labourers, such as Jonathan Whitehorne, who worked on the pesthouses for the standard labourers' rate of 1s.6d. per day.[5] But it is also likely that many of those described as waterman accepted any labouring work available, as several examples of men described both as waterman and labourer suggest,[6] and therefore that the importance of the river is somewhat overstated. On the other hand, the fact that such men were usually described as watermen rather than labourers, unlike at Wandsworth and Richmond, may indicate that the river provided more of their work than it did elsewhere.

To take the analysis further it is necessary to distinguish between trades which brought employment to Putney and those which merely served Putney's population. Any settlement will have a significant proportion of its people in the food, building and clothing trades, but it is not these which cause a settlement to grow in the first place. With this in mind, five main sources of employment in Putney can be identified. One, obviously, was water transport, discussed already.

A second was agriculture. Intensive agriculture, especially market gardening on the more fertile gravel soils towards the Thames, was greatly stimulated by the

Fig. 28 (left). The inventory of Henry Crane, husbandman (No. 130), compiled in 1679. It records two ground floor rooms and two above, all with fire equipment, corresponding to his four hearths in 1665. It lists his farming equipment, the most valuable items among which were eight horses and two colts (£43), nine cows and two calves (£30), corn (£65), hay (£35) and four dung heaps (£20).

nearness of London. Nevertheless, agriculture accounted for only about 17% of those working in Putney – not very different from Wandsworth and Richmond (20% and 11% respectively, plus some of the labourers). On the other hand, agriculture must also have provided work for the blacksmith, farrier, wheelwright and wharfinger (who dealt with dung brought from London to spread on the fields), as well as for some of the watermen. Market gardening was a relatively recent arrival in 1665,[7] and those listed in that year were probably the pioneers in Putney. Evidence from the 1680s suggests that the gardeners' holdings were typically 12 to 20 acres, compared with about 50 acres for husbandmen on the less fertile land.[8] One of the most important husbandmen was Henry Crane, on Putney Hill (Fig. 28), whose farming stock in 1679, valued at £221, included eight horses, 11 cows, ten pigs, ten acres of turnips, an acre of parsnips, corn, hay and four extremely valuable dung heaps, worth £20.

There is little direct evidence of farming being combined with other occupations, except in the cases of a few labourers and one victualler, though some of the watermen are likely to have worked on the land too. Very few people other than gentlemen, merchants, husbandmen and gardeners are recorded owning or leasing land other than house plots; in some of these cases the land was perhaps used for part-time farming (Richard Foster, waterman, William Garrett, waterman and George Giles, victualler), whereas in others the land was probably required for their acknowledged trade (John Hayes, poulterer and William Cobbett, butcher). Also, the inventories, other than those of husbandmen, rarely record livestock apart from the occasional horse or pig, though again there are a few exceptions – Ellen Jones had a cow and a milkhouse in 1669,[9] Grissell Jennings of Roehampton had three cows, a bullock and a calf in 1673 (and tubs and milk vessels) and Henry Driver, victualler, had a cow in 1682. Some of these may have been using the grazing rights on the commons belonging to the longer-established cottages – apparently one cow and calf, one mare and colt and one pig.[10] But it seems clear that most farming in Putney was a full-time activity.

A third source of employment was the great houses, which employed a large number of servants directly (who do not of course appear in the 1665 list or the table above) and also generated work for watermen and for specialised tradesmen such as Edward Jones the locksmith and Henry Tunstall the glasier. John Wright (No. 50) was described by Sir Thomas Dawes in 1648 as 'my waterman', and John Carpenter (No. 48) was referred to in exactly the same way by Edward Buckley esquire in 1680.[11] In 1668 Dawes

Fig. 29a & b. Token issued by Robert Jackson, tallow chandler (No. 40), in 1657, showing candle-making.

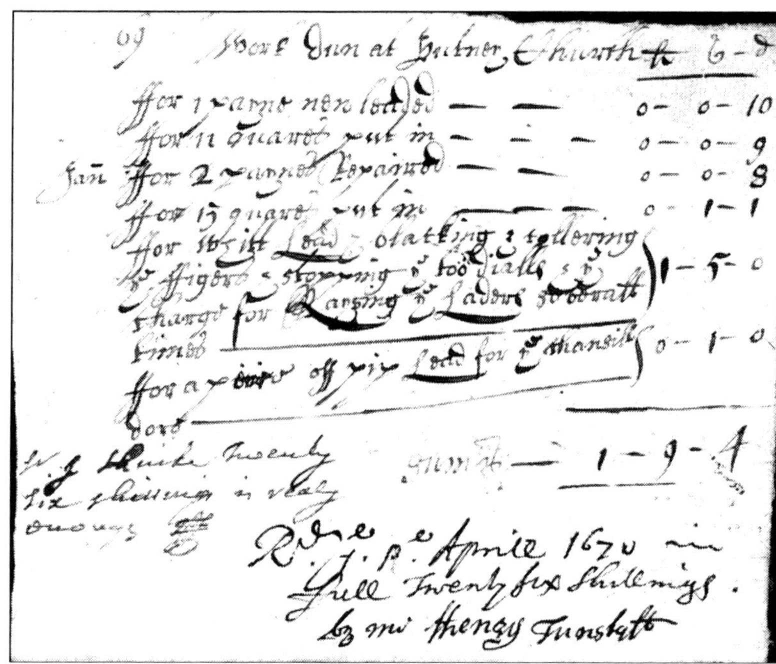

Fig. 30. A tradesman's bill, submitted by Henry Tunstall, glasier (No. 184) for work on the church in 1669. Tunstall claimed 29s. 4d, but someone (probably a churchwarden) has written on it 'I thinke twenty six shillings is realy enough', and Tunstall's receipt at the bottom is for that amount.

Wymondsold paid for eight servants to sit in a gallery in the church, but probably few had so many; two examples later in the century are of five servants and six servants (including a coachman and a gardener in the former case).[12] Assuming an average of five servants in each gentleman's or merchant's house, these household servants accounted for about a tenth of Putney's population. In 1665 they included 'Edward Dedford, a blak' at John Turner's house, one of a number of black servants recorded in seventeenth-century Putney.[13]

A fourth source of employment was road transport, which was more important than the table above suggests, since it also brought custom to the inns and alehouses and provided work for the blacksmith. The route by river from London to Putney and then by road up the Hill towards Portsmouth (or by road and then the cross-river ferry at Putney, which could carry a coach and horses)[14] was an important one, and so was the present A3 across the common.

The fifth (relatively minor) was production for a wider area than Putney. The main example of this was James White's brewhouse in Brewhouse Lane, dating back to medieval times.[15] White must have employed the coopers, drayman and others (his will of 1670 was witnessed by Andrew Weller of the Red Lion and John Mowden, cooper).[16] William Young, basketmaker, may also have supplied a wider area, no doubt using osiers (willow shoots) from the riverside at Putney or the Wandle mouth in Wandsworth, in both of which places they continued to be grown until the nineteenth or early twentieth century.

The two schoolmasters could also be placed in the category of providing goods or services for a wider area. Noah Bridges' school for boys probably existed from 1647 until his death in 1672, and Henry and Mary Portman's school for girls from 1638 or earlier possibly until 1702. The Portmans' school was 'for the education and breedinge upp of younge gentlewomen and for teachinge of them their needle and other things fitt for them to learne'; they boasted of having 'lords knights and

Fig. 31. The house in Lower Richmond Road known in the seventeenth century as the Barber's Apron, to which Henry Portman moved his girls' school in about 1664. It was one of the largest houses in Putney, with 18 hearths in 1665. It was just east of the present Waterman Street, where Kenilworth Court now stands.

gentlemens daughters of good repute and esteeme to bee schollers'. The fee in the 1640s was £18 per year, equivalent to the rent of a largish house, a farm or an inn in Putney; instruction in music, writing and dancing was an extra £6 or £7 per year.[17] Samuel Pepys' diary records in 1667 a visit to Putney church, 'where I saw the girls of the schools, few of which pretty'.[18]

The four poulterers are an interesting group. Their role seems to have been to gather produce from Surrey markets for consumption in Putney, though it is possible that they also sold produce in London. They are recorded breaching market regulations at Reigate, Guildford and Chertsey, and John Mascall junior was accused of fathering a child at Dorking.[19] In 1677 Goodwife Hayes was supplying Martha Turner at one of the large houses with not just eggs and chicken but also cheese, butter, bread, lamb, geese, veal, ducks, pigeons, pork, bacon and rabbits.[20] John Mascall senior prospered sufficiently to acquire a reasonably substantial landholding in Putney, including the eight cottages on the corner of Felsham Road in 1669.[21]

With the information above about occupations it is no mystery why Putney was growing. London was itself growing rapidly,[22] which stimulated river and road traffic and intensive agriculture, notably market gardening. It also encouraged the building of large houses for merchants and others, and several such houses were recent additions in 1665. Putney's growth was a reflection of London's.

Women's work

Much less is known about women's occupations than men's. In general there was a firm dividing line between the two in the seventeenth century.[23] However, widows sometimes continued their husband's trade, and two who clearly did, and were described as such, are included in the figures above – Hester Symonds, butcher, and widow Hayes, poulterer; so are Mary Marquis at the Wheatsheaf and Dorothy Burges, widow of a baker and apparently continuing to occupy the same premises.

Otherwise women tended to be confined to occupations such as the needle trades, charring, hawking and personal services such as nursing.[24] One such employment was especially important in Putney, as in other parishes around London: taking in children from London for wet nursing in the relatively healthy country air.[25] Putney's air was regarded as particularly good, and it says a great deal for its quality that in 1659 Alexander Vincomb, esquire, was willing to entrust his son Theophilus to the care of William Young, basketmaker, in Thundering Alley. Inevitably, many such children died in Putney and are therefore recorded in the parish register, which reveals that at least 45 households listed in 1665 kept one or more nurse children between 1656 and 1675. Of these, 22 were headed by a waterman and two by the widow of a waterman. Six had one hearth (including five of the poorest households), 31 had two hearths (including 11 of the poorest) and eight had from three to six hearths. The characteristic sound in Putney must have been a crying child.

Another employment, prostitution, is suggested by the accusation made in 1664 by Henry Driver, constable, against Margery, wife of Edward Matthews, waterman (No. 78, probably in Pepper Alley) and others, 'being taken by him in the night tyme togeather with severall others of evill and loose bahaviour as common night walkers'.[26] Also, as indicated above, several women kept a cow or two, and at least one spun shoemakers' thread.

Watermen's widows, or their wives in their absence, were sometimes supported by an apprentice: in 1669, for example, the Vestry agreed to pay widow Combes 18d. per week 'untill she getts a servant to worke & gett something for her', and in 1673 the pension of William Holton's wife (Holton having been press-ganged into the Navy) was terminated 'by reason shee hath a prentis now that works for her'.[27] The parish authorities certainly expected women to work if capable of doing so: the pension of Margery Deane (No. P5) was ended in 1673 not just because she refused a place in the almshouse but because 'shee is able to worke'.[28]

An isolated community?

Analysis of Putney's occupations rules out any idea of Putney being an isolated community lacking knowledge of the wider world. All the inhabitants of the largest houses spent much of the year in London, to which most of their servants will have accompanied them. The watermen travelled up and down the river, no doubt talking to their passengers on the way. The inns and alehouses depended on the travellers passing through Putney. The poulterers attended distant markets, and the gardeners probably sold much of their produce in London. Putney was as open to outside influences as anywhere in England.

An indication of Putney's horizons is provided by the residences of marriage partners given in the parish register in 1653-60: in 19 cases both partners were from

Putney parish, but ten marriage partners of Putney people were from London (including Westminster and Southwark), four were from Fulham, four were from nearby places in Surrey (Mortlake, Barnes, Malden and Ewell) and four were from further afield.

Roehampton

Information about occupations in Roehampton is very incomplete, but two sources of employment evidently dominated. One was the Great House and the other large houses. Their construction, largely in the 1620s, is undoubtedly the reason why the number of houses in Roehampton had doubled since 1617. The other was agriculture, though Roehampton had little or no land suitable for market gardening, and most of those who farmed were described as husbandmen. There were two carpenters, two innholders, a brickmaker, a farrier, a baker and a tailor, but otherwise virtually no non-agricultural employments.

Putney parishioners in trouble at Surrey quarter sessions, 1664-7

Nicholas Waxham: left Putney, leaving two children chargeable to the parish; his father, Nicholas Waxham (206), claims he is unable to keep them.
Nicholas Waxham, tailor: hunting a deer in New Park [Richmond Park].
John Hayes, poulterer (117): forestalling and engrossing fowls and rabbits in Reigate market [these were offences against market regulations].
Robert Overton, victualler: keeping a disorderly house.
John Mascall, Thomas Denning, Richard Foster & Thomas Bryan (96, 95, 63, 15): not submitting accounts as surveyors of the highways.
Robert White, innholder (207): erecting a cottage without four acres.
Alice Broome/Browne, spinster: beating Ellen Gurney (guilty); to keep the peace towards her. Elizabeth, wife of John Anderton, labourer (132), & Elizabeth, wife of John Sergeant, husbandman (139): to keep the peace towards Ellen Gurney.
Robert Jackson, chandler (40): using false weights (guilty).
Robert Miles (137), William Mabbs & Nicholas Smith (195), victuallers: keeping common alehouses without licence (guilty).
Thomas Seers, waterman (50A): plying his boat between Putney and London on Sundays (guilty).
Margery Mathews (78), Elizabeth James and Thomas Alexander: being common night walkers.
Thomas Mabsden, wheelwright (127): to keep the peace towards Mary Mabsden.
Richard Clarke, waterman, and wife Anne (89): to keep the peace towards Thomas Seers, waterman, and wife Anne (and vice versa).
John Robins of Putney Park, gentleman (129B): allowing ditches by the highway to Richmond to overflow.
Henry Burnham, cooper (43): to keep the peace towards Elizabeth Burnham.
John Mascall junior, poulterer & Frisweed, wife of John Mascall senior, poulterer (77, 96): telling two justices of the peace, 'You are rogues and rascalls and pittyfull fellowes'.
Richard Kestway, William Dove [Doe?], Nicholas Beagent (205) & William Platt, bakers: selling under-weight penny loaves (all except Dove fined).
John Mascall junior, poulterer (77): forestalling chickens at Guildford.
Richard Broughton, waterman & wife Elizabeth (188): not attending church for a month (gaoled for refusing to plead) [they were Quakers].
George Giles, victualler (124): keeping a house for illicit games, namely dice, cards and tables.
Thomas Denning, carpenter (95): allowing his wharf to be out of repair.

Source: QS.
Note: Numbers relate to the directory. Only in a few cases is it known whether those accused were found guilty.

Plate 1. Sir John Lawrence (d.1692), Lord Mayor of London in 1665 and occupant of the mansion called Coalecroft. The Lawrences owned Coalecroft from 1656 to 1711. The portrait is attributed to Gerard Soest.

Plate 2. Putney's riverside, seen from the bridge in about 1750 – the earliest known view of Putney. The bridge and some of the buildings shown had been built since 1665, but Putney's general appearance would have been familiar to the inhabitants of 1665.

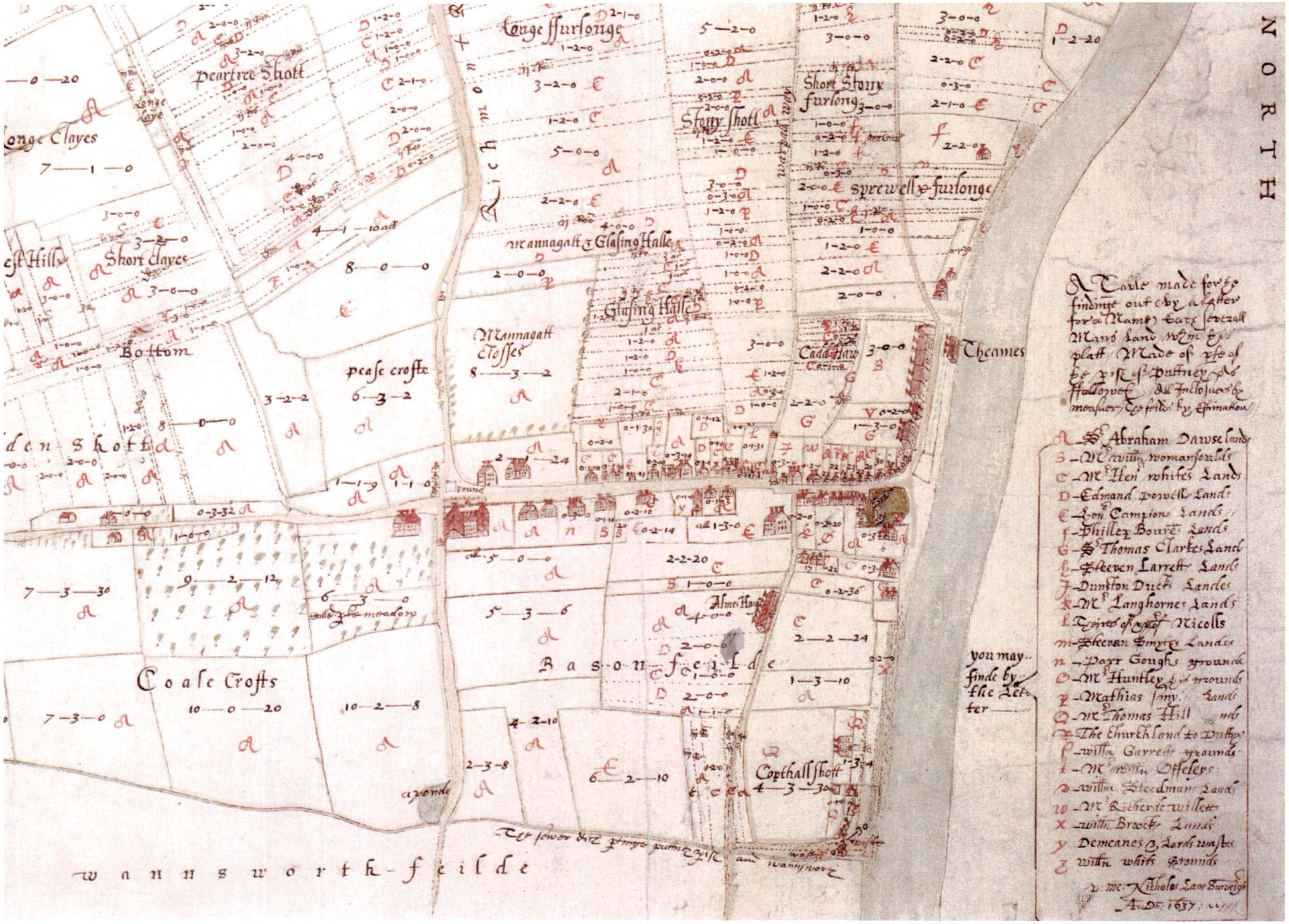

Plate 3. Nicholas Lane's map of Putney in 1636, showing the buildings concentrated in the High Street and the nearby river-side.

Plate 4. John Pettiward (d. 1671), merchant and London Alderman, painted by Gerard Soest in about 1650. Pettiward obtained his Putney property through his marriage in 1630 to Sarah, daughter of Henry White of Putney (d. 1658). His family continued to occupy Fairfax House, Putney, until about 1810, and they still own property in Putney.

Plate 5. St Mary's church, Putney, seen from the south-east in 1797. From the left are the porch added in 1623, dormer windows lighting the galleries, the tower of about 1500, the stairs to Henry Portman's gallery, Bishop West's chantry chapel of about 1530, and the chancel. The church was rebuilt in 1836, but the tower and (on new sites) the chantry chapel and the columns inside have survived.

Plate 6. Henry White (c.1584-1658), baker, money-lender and landholder of Putney, seen here in 1654 aged 70. He holds his wand of office as High Sheriff of Surrey. On White's death, his lands passed to his daughter Sarah and her husband John Pettiward, founding the Pettiwards' fortunes in Putney.

Plates 7 & 8. Eliab Harvey (1598-1661), merchant, and his wife Mary (1607-73). Eliab moved to a mansion in Roehampton in about 1640, purchasing it in 1654. After his death the property passed to his son William, but Mary continued to live there as well.

5. The houses

Information is available about the houses from probate inventories, which list the possessions of a deceased person, often room by room. To some extent they provide a check on the hearth tax information, but not reliably, as they rarely coincide in date with the hearth tax list (so houses could have been altered and occupants might even have moved house), hearths were recorded only if there was fire equipment in the room (and in summer it might be stored elsewhere), and rooms might be omitted altogether if they contained nothing belonging to the deceased. Inventories are therefore likely to under-record hearths. They are nevertheless useful in showing what a particular number of hearths actually meant in terms of rooms, and in demonstrating that, for the smaller houses, the number of hearths was as much a measure of comfort as it was of the size of the dwelling or the wealth of the occupant.

The great houses

Putney's great houses ranged from Elizabethan ones such as Portman's school (Fig. 31) and the White House (Figs. 33 and 34) to modern brick houses such as John Turner's (Nos. 17, 144 and 121 respectively). Inventories survive for all three of the largest. The largest of all, Dawes Wymondsold's (Fig. 32), had 37 hearths even after some reduction in its size in the 1650s, making it comparable to Osterley and Swakeleys (39 hearths each) and much larger than Ham House and Kew Palace (27 and 25 hearths). It was an H-shaped brick house, built in 1635-6, and later fire insurance records indicate that it had three storeys plus garretts above.[1] The inventory, of 1675, starts on the ground floor, with three parlours, withdrawing room, hall, waiters' hall, kitchen and other offices. On the floor above – evidently the principal floor, with most of the show rooms – were chambers, including the best chamber, and also dining room and drawing room. Apparently another floor up, perhaps occupying most of the space, was the upper gallery, as well as the study, balcony chamber and wardrobe chamber. Up again were the garretts, where the servants probably slept (one was 'the maids chamber'). There were also cellars and outbuildings.

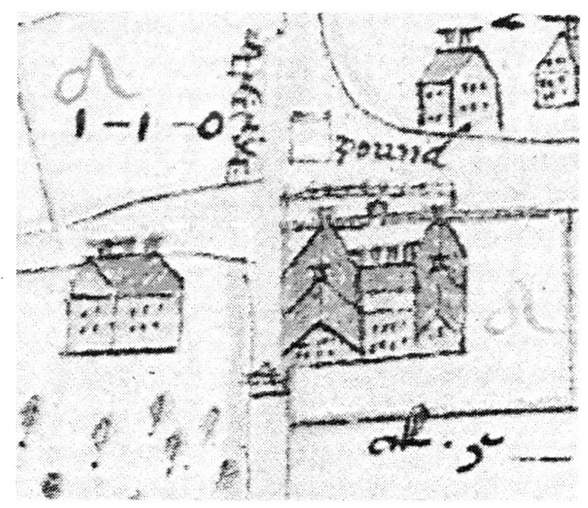

Fig. 32. Dawes Wymondsold's house, as shown on Lane's map in 1636. On the left is Coalecroft.

The house was richly furnished, with, for example, gilt leather hangings and a statue in the ground-floor withdrawing room and 26 pieces of tapestry distributed between the best chamber, the chamber over the black parlour, the dining room, the damask chamber, the chamber over the still house and the

Fig. 33. The White House (later known as Essex House), occupied in 1665 by Sir Thomas Chamberlayne (No. 144). It had 16 hearths. The house had been built in the 1590s by John Parr, embroiderer, and survived, though re-fronted and altered, until 1872. Sainsbury's supermarket now stand on its garden.

Fig. 34. The back of the White House, which was less altered than the front.

Fig. 35. House later known as Fairfax House (No. 147), on the east side of the High Street, seen from its garden in about 1880. Much of the 20-hearth house occupied by John Pettiward in 1665 was rebuilt in about 1700 (the part on the right), but the part on the left, with its massive chimneys and leaded windows, had evidently survived from the house built by Henry White in the 1630s.

Fig. 36. A half-timbered house in Putney Bridge Road, formerly the home of the Campion family and later known as Cromwell House (No. 152). In 1665 it was occupied by William Throckmorten, a merchant, and had 11 hearths.

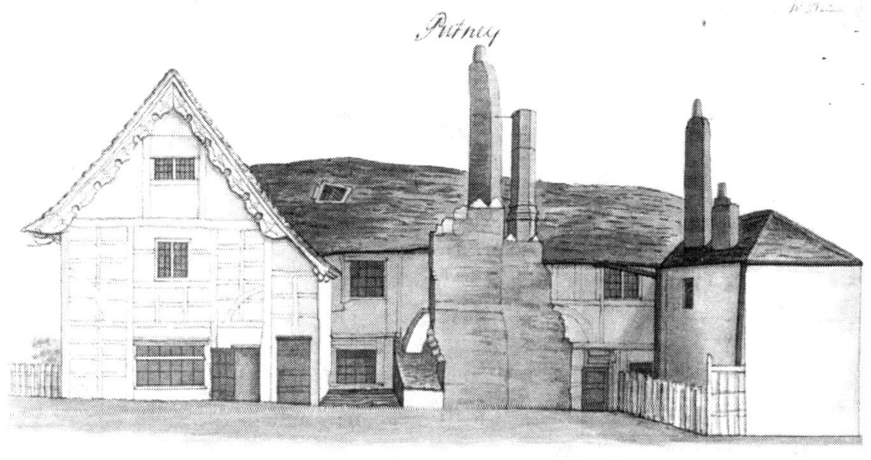

Fig. 37. Another view of Cromwell House.

Fig. 38. The house later known as Clyde House, on the south side of Lower Richmond Road (No. 24), seen from across the road in 1882. There was a great house here from the time of Henry VIII or earlier. It was briefly occupied by Captain John Blunt in 1665, and had 13 hearths. It was subdivided in the late 1670s, and part of it, including a gallery on the left-hand side, was destroyed.

Fig. 39. Clyde House seen from the Thames in 1873, showing the tall central section and two gabled wings.

wardrobe chamber. The great parlour was large enough for 28 chairs and stools and two tables, and the dining room for 21 chairs and two couches; even the study contained 16 chairs and stools, together with a pair of globes. The later fire insurance records refer to four marble chimneypieces and five Portland stone chimneypieces. By 1719 the house had been divided into two large dwellings, and it was demolished in 1788, unfortunately without anyone having drawn it.[2]

The second-largest house, Sir John Lawrence's at the foot of the Hill, with 31 hearths, is recorded in inventories of 1655 and possibly 1692. In 1655, when William Langhorne, merchant, occupied it, it seems to have been similar in arrangement to Wymondsold's, with parlours, hall, kitchen and other offices on the ground floor, chambers together with dining chamber and probably the great chamber on the first floor, and the long gallery and other chambers on the floor above, though the number of floors is unclear. The 1692 inventory may have been of the same house rather than a new one, though if so the long gallery had been divided into garretts. At both dates the house was richly furnished. In 1692 the furnishings of the chamber at the head of the great stairs (including 'a blew velvitt bed lined with white satten imbroydered') were valued at £102, out of a total of £546 for household goods.

Peter Proby's house (No. 143), on the site of Disraeli Road, with just 12 hearths (the inventory indicates 11), had a similar plan on a smaller scale: kitchen and other offices, three parlours and hall on the ground floor, chambers, wardrobe, closets and 'long dyneing roome' above and garretts. Some of the names of rooms indicate the decoration, such as the gilt leather room and the green drugget room, and the dining room and widow's chamber had tapestry hangings (ten pieces in total). In the garden were two statues. Cordwell Hammond's house (No. 52), with only nine hearths, was simpler, with just kitchen and offices, hall, parlour, four chambers and two garretts. In Hammond's garden were a banqueting house, a stone roller and a hammock.

Lesser houses

Lower down the social scale, the typical house had two hearths. The inventories indicate that this usually meant a two-room ground-plan, with parlour and kitchen on the ground floor, two chambers above and a garrett or garretts, as in the case of Edward King (No. 180); in this example only the kitchen and parlour were heated. Variations in the two-room plan included replacement of the parlour by a shop (Joan Juer, Fig. 42), a third chamber on the second floor (James Emberton, No. 56), and an extra room (perhaps no more than a lean-to) on the ground floor and a hall instead of a parlour (Nicholas Gladwyn, No. 230).[3] Kitchens usually (but not always) contained a table and chairs, and so were presumably used for eating as well as cooking. Kitchens and parlours rarely contained beds. Few houses had a hall.

These two-hearth houses must sometimes have been crowded. No doubt some accommodated only a widow living alone, but others had many more occupants. For example, at the second house visited by plague in July-August 1665, Thomas Howell's in Brewhouse Lane (No. 169), the victims were his wife, two daughters, a lodger, a parish child and a nurse child. With Howell himself that was seven people, apart from any others who survived and so were not recorded.[4] In other houses there were servants or apprentices. Even in a one-hearth house like that of Thomas Seers, waterman (No. 50A), there could be a manservant,[5] who presumably assisted his master as a waterman.

The two-room ground plan was by far the most common arrangement, unlike in London's suburbs,[6] but there is one example of a two-hearth house with a one-room plan: in 1681 Daniel Constant (No. 20) had a kitchen, whose contents included a bed, a wainscoat partition and kitchen equipment (but no table); a chamber up one pair of stairs, with another bed and a table and chairs; and a garrett, again with a bed.[7] Kitchen and chamber were heated. In the chamber were 'ye hangings of ye

Fig. 40. A house on the east side of the High Street, which from its style was probably standing in 1665. It must have been part of the nine-hearth house held by the owner of the tithes (No. 148).

Fig. 41. A house on the north side of Lower Richmond Road, immediately west of Spring Passage. From its style, the house may have been standing in 1665 (about No. 2), though it cannot be traced in the manor court rolls.

Fig. 42. The end of the row of eight cottages on the northern corner of the High Street and Felsham Road, seen from the High Street in about 1881. The windows (pre-dating sash windows) indicate that the cottages survived long enough to be photographed. The one visible is Thomas Juer's two-hearth cottage (No. 55, later Joan Juer's), with kitchen, shop, two chambers over them and garretts above.

roome & pictures' (valued at only 1s.). The Constants had five children between 1663 and 1672 (and no burials are recorded until 1675) and they had a manservant in 1674, so the house was certainly crowded. Nevertheless the Constants were reasonably well off, Daniel's widow Dorothy having £11 in cash and the lease of an alehouse in 1683.

Not many inventories are available for those with from three to six hearths, but those there are suggest that at least the three and four-hearth houses were often similar in plan to those with two hearths. For example, Richard Fisher (No. 106), with four hearths indicated in the inventory rather than the six listed in 1665, had kitchen, parlour, chambers over each of them and a 'passage room', all but the latter being heated. Henry Crane (No. 130), with four hearths, had kitchen, room by it, and two chambers above, again all heated. Thomas Pannett (No. 190), with three hearths, had shop and kitchen, chambers over (one with a closet) and garretts. These examples indicate that the number of hearths was often more an indication of comfort than of size of house. On the other hand, Henry Driver (No. 181), with four hearths in 1665, had kitchen, parlour and little room on the ground floor and three chambers over them, though the inventory records fireplaces only in the kitchen, the parlour and one of the chambers.

Houses were more likely to have a greater proportion of heated rooms, especially upstairs chambers, if more recently constructed, and above all if built of brick, or at least having had brick chimneys added. It was normally only brick chimneys which had fireplaces on upper floors; timber chimneys rarely did so.[8]

Two inventories record one-hearth houses. Occupants of such houses probably included the poorest in the parish, but not every one-hearth house was necessarily tiny or inhabited by the poor.[9] In 1673 Grissell Jennings (No. 254) in Cottage Row, Roehampton, had a kitchen (with five stools and two cupboards), a room by it (containing only beer tubs and milk vessels) and two chambers above (containing a bed in each and little else, except a trunk for clothing in the chamber over the kitchen); only the kitchen was heated. In other words the plan was similar to a standard two-hearth house, with four rooms. In contrast, in 1665 John Squibb (No. 226) had just two rooms: 'the first roome', evidently a kitchen, contained kitchen equipment and two chairs, two forms, a table, a cupboard and a 'hanging cupboard'; 'the second room' was evidently a bedroom, containing a bed and bedstead, form, chest, two trunks, two churns and three tubs. The kitchen presumably contained the hearth.

One other probable one-hearth house was inventoried in 1669, though the house cannot be located. Ellen Jones of Putney, widow, had a lower room

Fig. 43. A cottage known as Bear's Den Hall on the east side of Putney Hill (about where Kersfield Road is now) in about 1720. The view is somewhat fanciful, commemorating the cottage's use as a summer house by two eccentrics in the early eighteenth century, and artistic licence has undoubtedly been taken, but it may indicate what the poorest one-hearth cottages were like. It was written that the two occupants 'went up a ladder to a bedchamber, where there was only one bed, which served them both, & a small window where the head could hardly pass – thatched and no cieling'. The cottage was possibly the one occupied by John Butler, husbandman, in 1665 (No. 138). Not all one-hearth houses were as small and primitive as this.

(evidently a kitchen, with fire equipment, a table, three stools, a chest and a cupboard) and an upper room (evidently a sleeping chamber, with a bed and three chests).[10]

There is not much evidence of subdivision, and the inventories usually indicate a fairly regular arrangement of rooms, but there are a few examples, such as one of the houses in Thundering Alley (Fig. 22). The former farmhouse known as the Queen's Arms (Nos. 40-3) was divided into three parts by 1657, apparently at first because a former owner's widow was entitled to a third of it. By 1665 it accommodated four separate households, and the probably ramshackle structure helps explain how Henry Burnham could be convicted in 1668 of being 'a common evesdropper under the roofs of his neighbours, whereby many quarrels and controversies have arisen among his neighbours'.[11] The inventory of No. 29 in 1662 lists a low room (evidently the kitchen), another low room, three chambers and garretts, and one of the chambers was 'the chamber over Simonds house' (the neighbouring house being occupied by Symonds; see Fig. 49). The widows who occupied the two houses died of plague within about a week of each other in August-September 1665.

While every household in 1665 seems to have had at least one fireplace, Henry Vaughan and his wife were living by 1668 in what was described as a 'shed' (apparently newly-built). In that year the Vestry provided them with alternative accommodation, 'whereby his shed may be pulled downe which is soe very great annoyance to ye parishioners'.[12]

Building materials

Very few of the dwellings in Putney and Roehampton in 1665 survived long enough to be drawn or photographed. Probably most of them were constructed of wood, but brick had become increasingly common in the seventeenth century. In Roehampton there appear to have been just two brick houses in 1617, both recently built and one known as 'the brick house', indicating the rarity of brick then.[13] By the 1620s, merchants' and gentlemen's houses were routinely built of brick, such as the Great House and the house which became William Harvey's in Roehampton and, in the 1630s, Sir Abraham Dawes' house and Fairfax House in Putney. Indeed by 1623 bricks were being made at Roehampton, in the area between Ponsonby Road and Medfield Street.[14]

Use of brick took some time to percolate down the social scale, but a number of small brick dwellings of the 1650s or later in the seventeenth century survived long enough to be photographed, including Thundering Alley. The almshouse was also of brick. All the dwellings with heated chambers upstairs, such as Henry Crane's house, are likely to have been of brick, or at least to have had brick chimneys. Nevertheless, some dwellings continued to be built of timber – in Roehampton until the early nineteenth century.[15] It is also possible, though there is no direct evidence, that some of the lowest-quality housing, such as Cottage Row in Roehampton, was constructed even more simply of clay.

Some buildings in 1665 were thatched, probably using local straw or reeds. The last thatcher recorded in Putney was Thomas Kentish, who died in 1662; the last in Roehampton was one Harding, who died in 1656.[16] But the better-quality buildings are likely to have been roofed by tiles long before this. In about 1628 Sir Abraham Dawes established a tile kiln adjacent to Putney Heath, using clay from the common, though it is not known how long it continued.[17] Many of the older buildings recorded in nineteenth-century photographs were roofed with pantiles.

Rents

The information available on rents (from two rentals, lawsuits and the churchwardens' accounts) has to be treated with caution, since the annual rent may be affected by other terms in the lease, such as a large entry fine or an undertaking to rebuild, or by the condition of the property or by additional land covered by the lease. Also, there was probably a gradual rise in rents. However, there is sufficient information to obtain a reasonably clear picture.

Among the largest houses, the highest annual rent recorded was Henry Portman's £50, almost certainly for the 18-hearth house he occupied in 1665. For houses with 11 to 14 hearths, the rents were £20, £21 (with a £160 entry

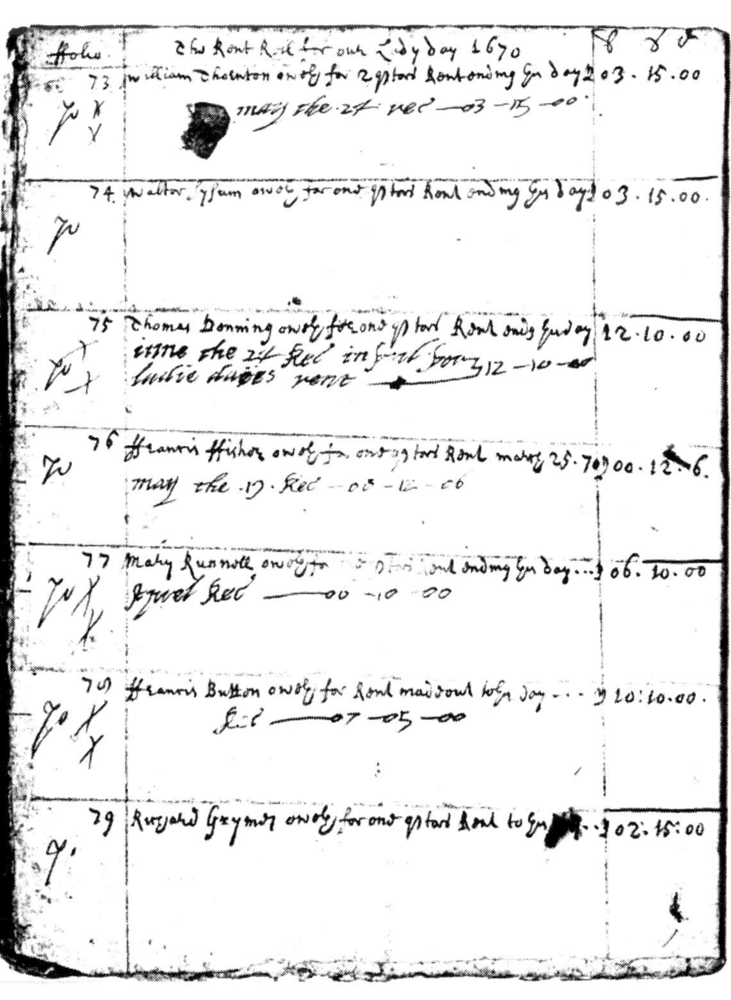

Fig. 44. A page from John Pettiward's rent book, showing rents due on Lady Day 1670, including those from Walter Sisam, Thomas Denning, Francis Fisher, Mary Runnell, Francis Button and Richard Grimes.

fine), £25, £30 and £33 (with no entry fine); £14 was paid for each of two nine-hearth houses. For four holdings including a house and farmland (two of them in Roehampton), the annual rents were £14, £14, £15 and £26.[18] For substantial houses of three to six hearths, the recorded rents were £3, £6, £10, £10-15, £13 and £20.[19] For two-hearth houses, John Fawdrie's rent, £12, was the highest recorded; rents for three others were from £2½ to £7.[20] A £5 rent would have accounted for a fifth of a labourer's wage if he obtained work six days a week throughout the year, but probably none were employed so continuously. In Roehampton's Cottage Row, the annual rents for two one-hearth cottages were £1.5s.0d. and £1.10s.0d. in 1660 and 1663; one room in a cottage by the churchyard wall in Putney was rented for a pauper for £1.10s.0d. a year in 1668; and the annual rent for one of the houses in Pepper Alley was £1.10s.0d. in 1673.[21] Other annual rents paid from 1664 to 1673 for those receiving poor relief were £1.10s.0d. in two cases and £1.4s.0d.[22] Hence the reaction of local justices of the peace when the Government tried to restrict exemption from the hearth tax to those occupying houses worth less than £1 per year: several signed a list in 1672 certifying 50 persons as exempt but adding 'as to the povertie, but not the rents of the above named persons'.[23]

Rents were much lower than in the City of London, where merchants' houses in the 1690s averaged £56 a year, the average paid by male householders was £25 a year and the cheapest houses were about £10 a year. On the other hand, typical rents in the East End and Southwark were between £3 and £5 a year.[24]

The hearths

What did the people of Putney burn in their hearths? In 1640 Sir Abraham Dawes left £50 to provide seacoal for the poor of Putney, and in 1670 coal was being purchased for the almshouse from John Lee at the wharf (No. 160).[25] The inventories most often mention coal, and fire equipment generally included tongs, which were needed for coal but not wood, but many inventories also mention wood (in John Hulke's case 'firewood').[26] For example Dawes Wymondsold in 1675 had three chaldrons of coal and five loads of wood, worth £6.15s.0d. At least some of the wood came from the commons.

6. Inns and alehouses

There were 17 dwellings occupied by innholders or victuallers in Putney in 1665 and two (or possibly three) in Roehampton, though two of the Putney ones were recorded as unlicensed. The numbers were almost the same as those when licensing records become available in the following century,[1] suggesting that the strict licensing system which controlled the numbers later was already in place in 1665.

They varied greatly in importance, from major inns to humble alehouses, and this is reflected in both hearths and rents. The four main inns (Nos. 31-3 and 136) had from ten to 12 hearths, and rents for three of them were £24, £24 and £20. The two Roehampton inns (the Three Stags' Heads and the White Hart) each had six hearths, and the rent for the former was only £5. The alehouses had from two to six hearths, and rents for seven of them ranged from £3 to £13. Andrew Driver at the White Hart near the heath gate, with two hearths, called himself an innholder but probably had no more than an alehouse; he received a pension as a maimed soldier, and had presumably been injured in the Civil Wars. Inns were generally more respectable than alehouses and provided a wider range of services, sometimes becoming the centre of upper-class social life, but even alehouses were expected to provide lodging as well as drink.

Three of the most important inns were clustered together near the ferry landing: these were the Red Lion, the White Lion and the Bull, together with lesser establishments known as the Wheatsheaf and the Falcon. The Red Lion was the most important of them, where the entire parish assembled once a year for a meal on the day of perambulating the parish boundaries.[2] It was unusual in having a licence to sell wine,[3] and its occupant, Andrew Weller, was described as a vintner rather than an innholder. For the White Lion a detailed inventory survives, though it apparently omits the innholder's own accommodation. There were ten named rooms: the Moon, the Star, the King's Head, the Queen's

Figs. 45a & b and 46a & b. Trade tokens issued by James Russell of the Falcon in 1667 (No. 34) and by John Lee of the Anchor in 1668 (No. 160).

Head, the Castle and the Bull Head contained beds, but the Sun, the Crown, the Lion and the Rose contained only tables and chairs, and were perhaps dining rooms. The Lion seems to have been the best room, with 'fifteene hangings of greene stript stuffe' and Spanish tables. The Rose had 'men for gameinge'.

A notable feature of James Russell's Falcon, at least by 1688, was 'the coffee roome', apparently on an upper floor. Whereas the White Lion had just beer and wine cellars, the Falcon had stocks of beer, brandy and coffee (worth £10).

Many of the other inns and alehouses were located to serve road traffic, including what had earlier been known as the Anchor, at the foot of the Hill, and the White Hart at the top of the Hill. On Putney Heath, the bowling alley and adjoining house was a major place of entertainment, where the Surrey justices of the peace were holding their monthly meetings by 1670.[4] Further on, in Putney Vale, was the White Hart or Halfway House, dating from the 1650s.[5] It was close to Richmond Park, and the innholder, John Hulke, described himself in 1686 as 'one of his Majesties groomes attending his said Majesties hunting horses', and stated that he had looked after horses of the King and his courtiers at the inn; there was even a door made in the park wall for him.[6] Serving a different form of transport was John Lee, wharfinger and victualler at the wharf in the north-east of the parish; his house was probably known as the Anchor, though the trade token he issued also shows three tuns. He was convicted in 1661, with others, of having 'kept and held unlawful games and [having] received and entertained their neighbours' servants at unlawful times, both by day and night, idly drinking, swearing and brawling, to the great disturbance of their neighbours'.[7]

At the majority of the alehouses victualling was the holder's main occupation, but sometimes victualling and another trade were combined, as at the Blue Anchor in the High Street, where Richard Grimes was described as a waterman. John Mowden in the High Street was both cooper and victualler, and his alehouse was evidently the one known as the Coopers' Arms, which survived until 1907. John Martin was both husbandman and victualler (though an unlicensed one in 1663), and his alehouse may have been the Half Moon, first recorded as such in 1723,[8] though the precise site of Martin's dwelling is uncertain.

Two of the inns or alehouses of 1665 have definitely continued to the present day – now known as the Walkabout (opposite St Mary's church) and the Fox (Nos. 32 and 124). Three others may also date back to 1665: the Duke's Head (first recorded by name in 1714, as the Duke of Ormonde's Head),[9] the Half Moon and the Green Man (built in about 1700[10] but possibly replacing the White Hart, which stood on a different site nearby) (Nos. 9, 61 and 133).

7. Office holding

In Putney, the Vestry elected four types of local official: churchwardens, who handled most parish affairs and finances; sidesmen, who were deputy churchwardens; overseers of the poor, who levied the poor rates and handled poor relief; and surveyors of the highways. The manor court elected three: constables, who had duties connected with public order; headboroughs, who were deputy constables; and aleconners, who dealt with weights and measures and the quality of foodstuffs.[1] In each case except constables there were two of each. The same officials were elected for Roehampton, but only one of each. Only for the overseer was there a property qualification (he was required to be 'a substantial householder').[2] Surveyors of the commons are recorded from 1669.

Churchwarden was the most desirable office, usually filled by the wealthy and hotly contested. When the churchwardens' accounts list unsuccessful candidates, from 1678 to 1694, there were sometimes as many as eight of them. A few of the less wealthy also served as churchwarden, including Edward Rogers, innholder, Walter Sisam, gardener and Henry Tunstall, glasier. The other office competed for was overseer of the poor, with up to six unsuccessful candidates in 1681-94. Occasionally someone of relatively high status was surveyor of the highways, or even constable (Henry Portman and Cordwell Hammond).[3] However, in the case of the constables there is evidence from the 1660s of someone other than the person elected – in fact Peter Rogers – carrying out the duties, presumably for a fee.[4]

The least prestigious offices were headborough and aleconner. Of the 22 householders who held only one office (apart from churchwarden), 12 were aleconner and five were headborough. Even a few of the poorest became aleconner, such as William Young, though the aleconners also included Robert Lewis, gentleman. Sometimes a progression is visible, for example in Daniel Constant's case from aleconner to headborough, sidesman and finally overseer of the poor. In 17 cases, those who held more than one office started as aleconner (only Peter Rogers became aleconner after holding another office), and it looks as if that office was used to test suitability for the more responsible posts. To understand how the choices were made, it would be necessary to know more about ages, length of residence in Putney and character, but there is a little evidence about ages. Among the 13 office-holders whose ages are known, eight were from 26 to 37 when they first held office, though the ages ranged up to 60.

In Roehampton, the same people tended to become churchwarden as held the other offices, and, as indicated above, most offices were confined to about 15 people. The poor were sometimes aleconner or headborough, and of the eight who held only one office four were aleconner and three headborough; four held those two offices only. The office of aleconner was used in the same way as in Putney, with 13 aleconners moving on to other offices.

8. The plague

The plague outbreak of 1665 probably killed more Londoners than any other, though the *proportion* of the city's population who died was higher in some earlier years.[1] The 1665 outbreak was also the last, and it affected the surrounding villages, spreading even to Roehampton. It was taking hold of London in June 1665, and plague deaths then rose to a peak in September, declining significantly from October. 15 to 20% of London's population died. A Putney householder, Sir John Lawrence, was Lord Mayor during the plague, and distinguished himself by remaining in the city, though he was reported as having a glass case constructed for himself, from which he supervised business and received visitors.[2]

Plague in Putney and Roehampton

In Putney plague first manifested itself on 22 July, and the first plague burial was on the following day.[3] Little is known about the first household affected,[4] but the second was, not surprisingly, that of a waterman. Most deaths were in August, September and October 1665, but the last was not until February 1667 (see Fig. 47 and Appendix 2).

The churchwardens' payments provide a more detailed picture. Goodwife Jones began nursing the sick on 22 July, and the account for building the pesthouses is dated 24 July. The allowance for the sick rose to a peak of 15s.6d. on 10-14 October, indicating 31 people in the pesthouses or shut up at home. It then declined rapidly to 5s.6d. per day at the end of November, indicating 11 people shut up, but, apart from a period of a month in February/March, did not fall below 3s. (six people shut up) until early June 1666, and payments continued until 22 August 1666. On 6 May 1666 the Vestry ordered that the

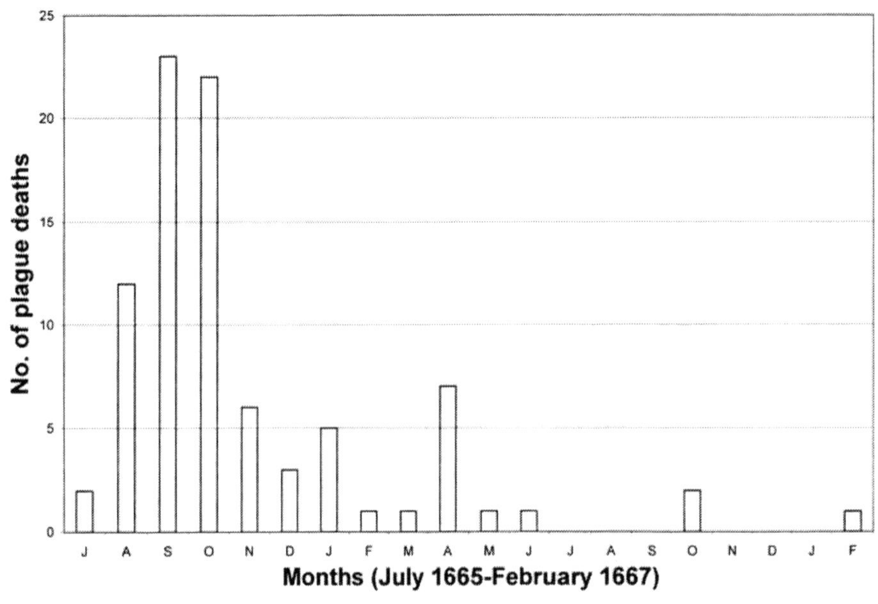

Fig. 47. Deaths from plague in Putney parish, 1665-7.

churchwardens 'do take care to provid a house for the removing of the visetted from the pest houses as soune as they can convenently'.[5] The last death was in the household of Richard Crane, bricklayer (No. 91): Crane's daughter Anne was buried on 29 November 1665, his sons Richard and Arthur on 11 and 26 October 1666 and his servant William Casement on 18 February 1667. Those who died seem to have been buried at Putney church (Francis Button's horse was hired to draw Robert Cooke's corpse there, and Henry Vaughan's horse to draw the body of Mowden's wife); graves continued to be dug (for example 20 'for ye infected' by Christopher Rogers in September 1665), and there is no indication of bodies being dumped in plague pits.

80 people died in Putney – about 7% of the population. The Roehampton deaths (seven in total) were from September to December 1665, accounting for perhaps 2% of Roehampton's population. The parish was affected relatively lightly. 'Excess mortality'[6] in 1665 was around 6 in suburban parishes close to the City of London, 4.6 within the City's walls, 3.9 in Wandsworth and only 3.0 in Putney parish.[7] In Wandsworth, where plague deaths continued to be numerous in 1666, 349 people died of the disease – 19% of the population, about the same proportion as in London itself.

Putney parish's 87 plague deaths occurred in up to 40 separate households.[8]

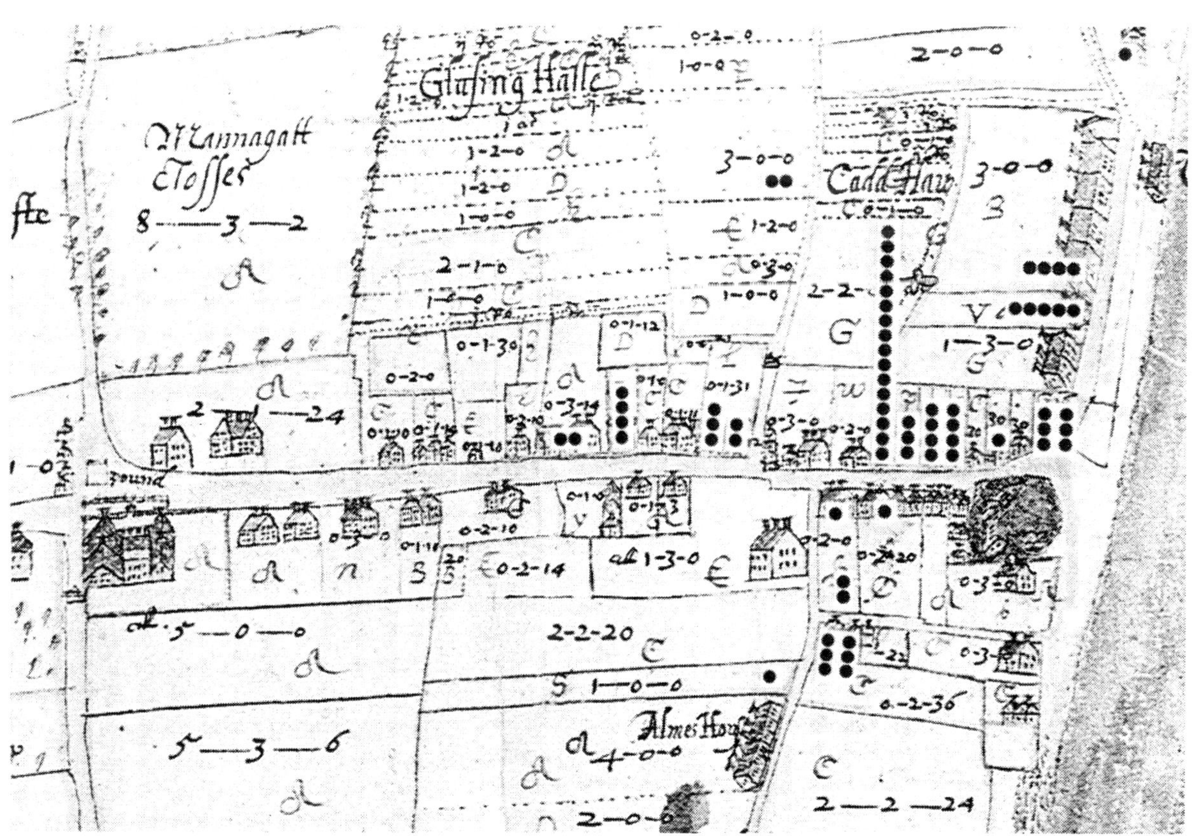

Fig. 48. Households in Putney where there were deaths from plague in 1665-7. Each round marker indicates one plague death. 68 of the 80 deaths in Putney are covered here. Of those which can be attributed to a household in the 1665 list, only one is off the map (at No. 129A).

Fig. 49. Sixteenth-century houses, evidently timber-built and much altered, on the south side of Lower Richmond Road at its junction with the High Street in about 1881. The photographer is standing outside St Mary's church looking along Lower Richmond Road. In 1665 the nearer one was occupied by Hester Symonds, butcher, with two hearths, and the further one by Susanna Cooke, widow of a waterman, with four hearths (Nos. 29-30). The two women died of plague within about a week of each other in August-September 1665, together with four members of their families. The inventory of Susanna's husband William, from 1662, records two low rooms on the ground floor (their lowness is clear from the photograph), one of these being a kitchen; three chambers above, one of them 'the chamber over Simonds house'; garretts; and a cellar.

Only in seven were there four or more plague deaths, and only in two were there six deaths: those of Thomas Howell senior, waterman, and William Young, basketmaker (Nos. 169 and 44). This pattern was similar to that in London, where almost two-thirds of affected households experienced only one death.[9]

The households affected by plague are shown on Fig. 48, in so far as they can be identified. Many of them were headed by watermen, who were obviously at particularly high risk, and whose households were certainly disproportionately affected (40% of the households headed by men, but 56% of the affected households headed by men).[10] Several people died at inns or alehouses, including the White Lion and the Wheatsheaf. The only deaths at houses with more than two hearths, other than inns and alehouses, were at Hester Symonds' and Henry Tunstall's. Occasionally the plague appears to have spread from one dwelling to its neighbour, as in the cases of Nos. 29 and 30 (a subdivided house – Fig. 49), Nos. 36, 37A and 39, and Nos. 45 and 46 (a subdivided house in Thundering Alley). The poor were affected disproportionately, but not massively so (45% of households, 61% of households with plague deaths, 59% of plague deaths).[11] Children were also disproportionately affected. Only four male heads of household died.

Dealing with plague

Putney was so dependent on London that it could not insulate itself from plague in the city. Restricting traffic through Putney, even if it had been possible, would have deprived the watermen and victuallers of their livelihoods. Even preventing Londoners sending children for nursing might have thrown some families into want, though the warrant obtained in November 1665 to remove a nurse child from Pharoah Clarke's may have been connected with plague. Church services continued to be held, despite the risk of assembling people together, and pitch was bought to burn in the church. In August John Hutchins was paid 1s.6d. 'for killing ye dogges' (stray animals being suspected of spreading plague).

The parish's most important action was to confine the sick in order to prevent the spread of infection. Pesthouses were built by Edward King on the edge of the Lower Common, as far as possible from any dwellings, for £19.5s.0d., plus £3.2s.0d. for the watchhouse. The total cost was £30.2s.11d., including 4s.4d. to Henry Tunstall for glass and 1s. to Mr Portman's maid for 'kitchen stuffe'. Goodwife Jones was the nurse from 22 July to the following 24 April, evidently managing not to become infected herself; at first she received the excellent salary of 10s. a week and from 22 January 5s. a week. She also searched people for signs of plague. Warders also had to be paid, at 7s. per week each.

Removing individuals to the pesthouse was presumably more economical than shutting up whole

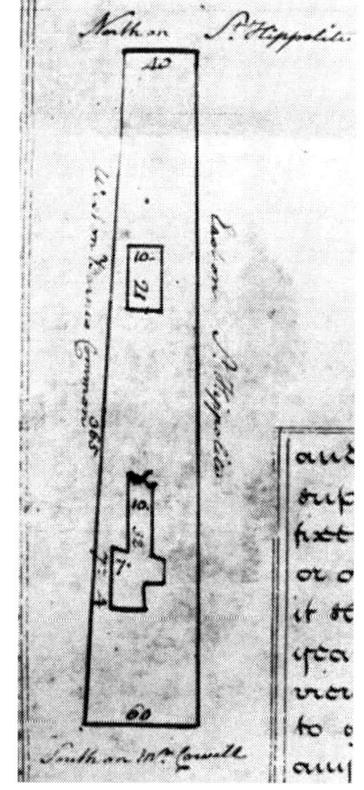

Fig. 50 (right). Plan of the pesthouses, from a deed of 1789. The pesthouses of 1665-6, unlike earlier ones, remained standing after the plague subsided and were let out as cottages. Earl Spencer leased the site to Putney parish, and the rent from the cottages was used to help the poor. Deeds indicate that there were three cottages and at the north end a wooden building.

Fig. 51. The pesthouses were finally taken down in 1862 and replaced by the six cottages shown here. 15 more cottages were added elsewhere on the site in 1880. The road is now known as Commondale.

households, but at least two households were shut up instead, probably because most of their members were infected. On 15 August 5s. was paid 'to Tho Howell senior when his house was shut up' (No. 169), and on 1 September 6d. 'to James Emberton when he shut up Rob Combes' (No. 20A). The grim task of removing people to the pesthouse also sometimes fell to Emberton; for example he received 1s.6d. on about 27 August 'when he removed wid Silley' (she was buried on 2 September). John Fawdrie's horse was several times borrowed for removing people. In 1666 it is possible to identify who was being removed to the pesthouse and when – for example three members of Hugh Williams' household when his son died on 22 February, four members of Thomas Char's household when daughter died on 26 March and three members of John Costrell's household when a boy from there died on 19 May (Nos. P1, 46 and 9). There was only one more death from these three households, and many of those removed to the pesthouses did in fact survive.

All this activity by the parish cost a great deal of money – £194 up to April 1666. This was raised by two voluntary subscriptions from the richer inhabitants (half the total), collections on regular fast days and additional poor rates. Once the outbreak was nearly over, the Vestry converted the pesthouses into three cottages and a wooden tenement, and they remained standing until 1862.[12]

Putney's experience of plague in 1665-7 is a reminder of its exceptional dependence on London. This close relationship with the city carried a heavy price in 1665-6, but it was what enabled Putney to grow and many of its inhabitants to prosper.

Part II

Directory of householders in 1665

Contents of the directory

The second, third and fourth columns provide the information given in the 1665 list, in the original order. Italics in those columns indicate householders omitted from the 1665 list but well-attested elsewhere; in all but three cases this information is from the 1664 hearth tax list.[1] The order of these added names in the table may not always be exact.

Name: The name, unless in italics, is as in the list of 1665. The more usual spelling, drawn from the parish registers, other hearth tax lists or other documents, is given in square brackets where necessary. Note that the landholder's name was sometimes listed if the property was empty, often with 'Ld' (expanded here to 'lord') after it.

Tax status: Unless in italics, this is from the 1665 list. As discussed above, *'poore' is not a reliable indication that someone was poor.* An asterisk in the table indicates that the householder was charged in 1664, and a cross that he or she paid rates in 1668, and therefore that (for tax purposes) they were almost certainly wrongly described as poor. Underlining of 'poore' indicates that the householder was exempted in 1664, when the criteria seem to have been applied more strictly. 'Ex' (short for 'examinatur') or various longer versions indicates that an entry from an earlier list had been examined by the collector and found correct; in the original list only these entries have figures in a separate column indicating the actual payments. 'Noe entr' presumably means that the house could not be entered to check the number of hearths, and 'noe distresse' (shortened here to 'noe d.') and 'nulla bona' presumably that it was not possible to distrain the goods of the householder concerned. Many dwellings were declared empty, one was 'not quite built' and one in Roehampton was 'burnt downe'.

H: This is the number of hearths, and (unless in italics) is from the 1665 list. A few blanks are filled in (in italics) from the 1664 list.[2]

Occupation: This is in brackets if deduced from possessions or activities rather than stated as an occupation. I indicates a nurse child between 1656 and 1675.

Status: The main item here is membership of the Vestry and election to parochial and manorial offices,[3] as follows:

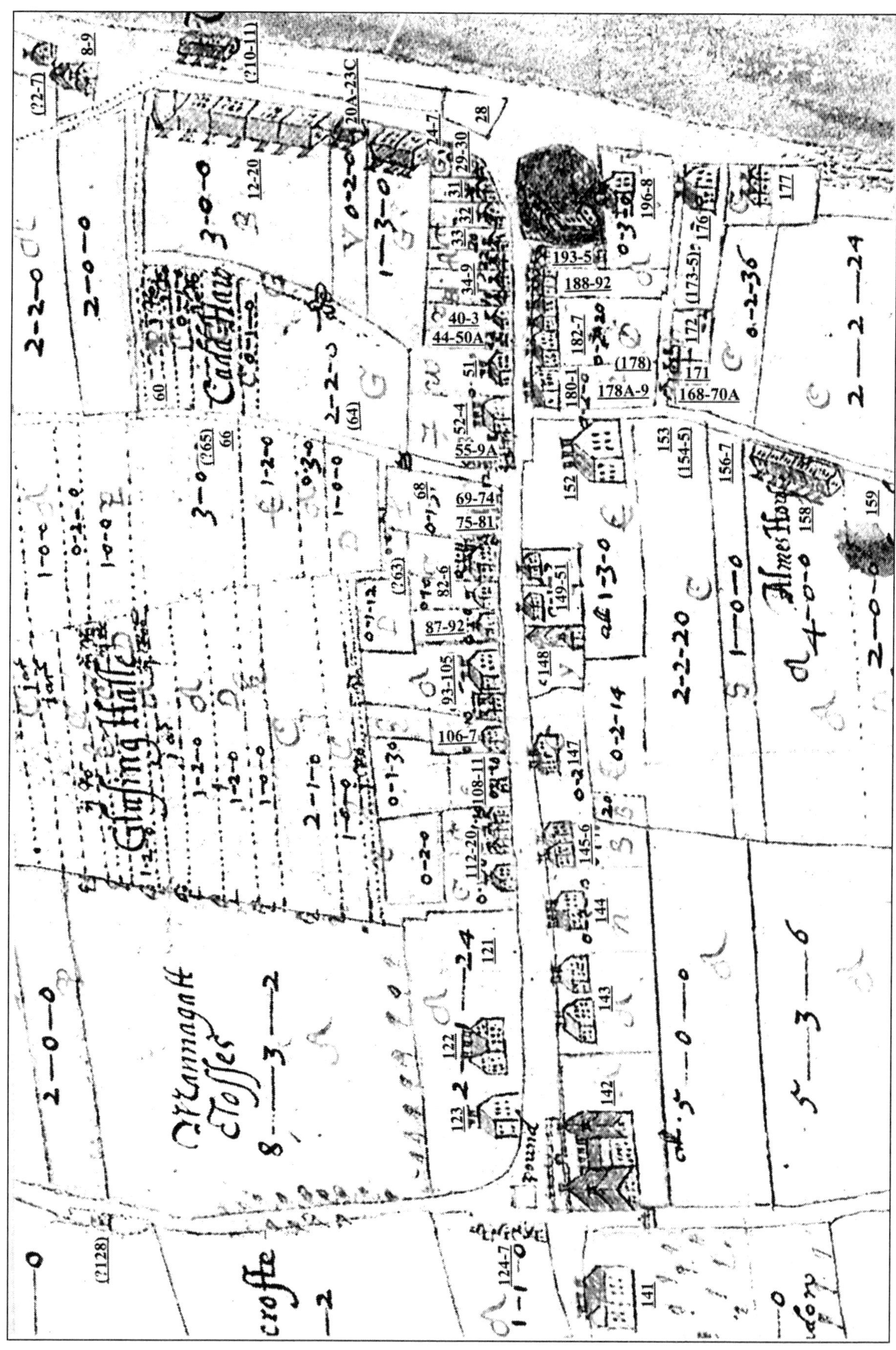

Fig. 52. Households in the hearth tax list for 1665 related to the 1636 map. Brackets around numbers indicate that the approximate location is known but not the exact site; a question mark indicates that the location is uncertain.

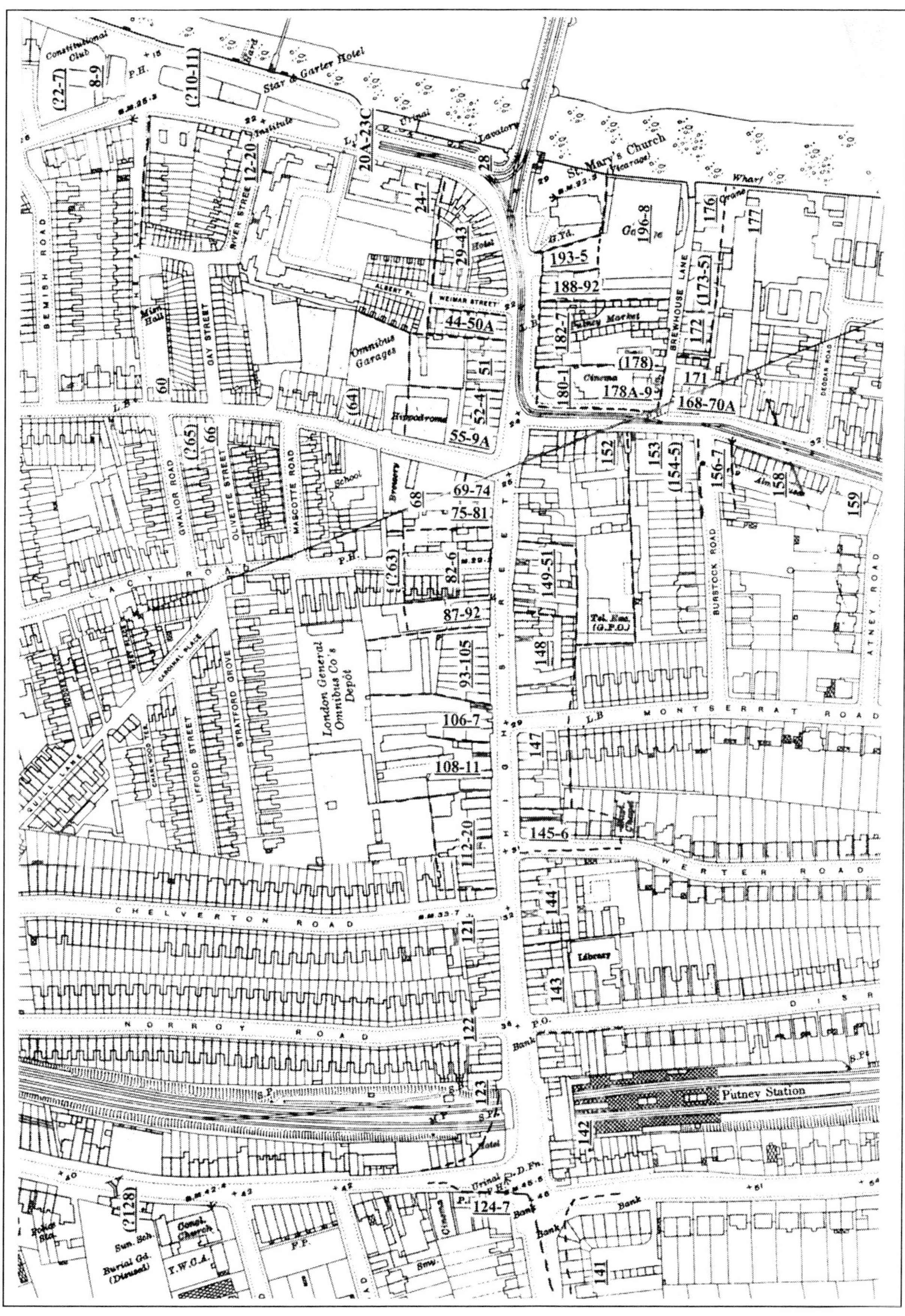

Fig. 53. Households in the hearth tax list for 1665 related to the 1913 Ordnance Survey map. Selected property boundaries of 1665 are marked by dashed lines.

Fig. 54. Households in Roehampton in 1665 related to the 1953 and 1964 Ordnance Survey maps. Only the minority of households which can be located even approximately are shown. Brackets and question marks are used as in Figs. 52 and 53. The village was then in what is now known as Roehampton Lane, but there was a row of small cottages along the north side of the present High Street, facing the Common, which later developed into what is now Roehampton village.

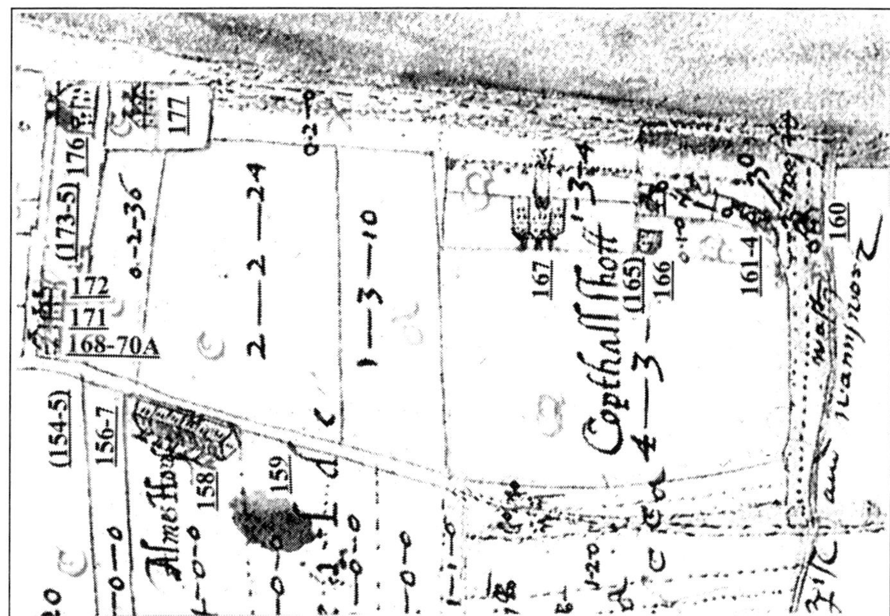

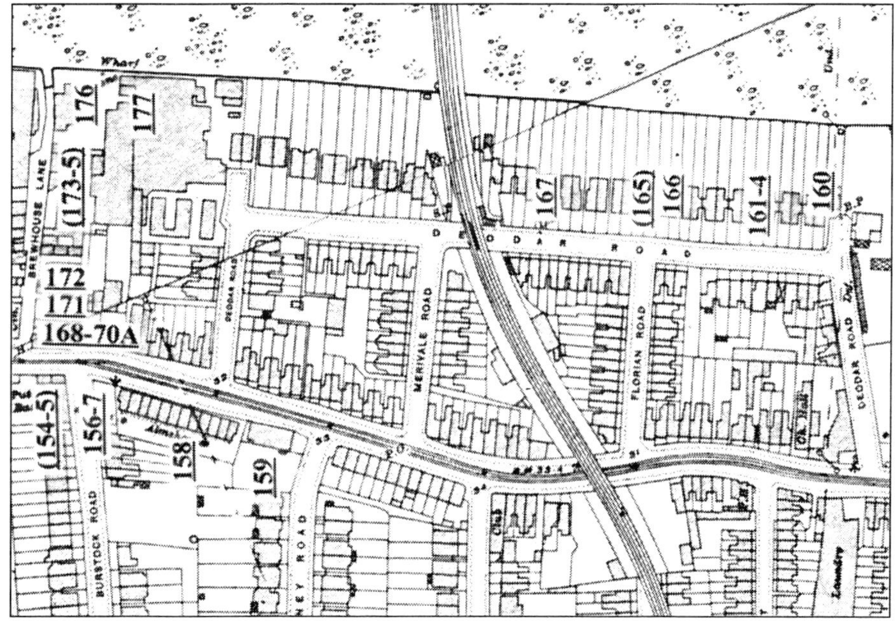

Figs. 55 & 56. Households of 1665 in the north-east corner of Putney parish related to the 1636 and 1913 maps.

CW – churchwarden
Side – sidesman
OP – overseer of the poor
SH – surveyor of the highways
Con – constable
Head – headborough
Ale – aleconner
C – supervisor of the commons.

'Pew' indicates the purchase of the right to a seat in the parish church; 'pew' is indicated even if only a pew for the householder's wife is recorded. Since rights to pews began to be sold on a much larger scale in 1668, householders who died before that date rarely had one. Information on pews is included here only up to

1668. 'Lit.' or 'Illit.' means literate or illiterate, and is based entirely on whether the person could sign his or her name. The number of plague deaths is indicated. Age in 1665 is given where known, and is probably not always precise. <R>, <C>, <P> and <P*> indicate rich, comfortable, poor and poorest – an impressionistic assessment based on number of hearths, holding of local offices and payments for pews.

Location: The property transfers summarised here name the householder in the 1665 list as occupier unless the contrary is indicated. Abuttals usually relate to the owner rather than the occupier of the neighbouring property. As regards inventories, rooms are given in the original order; an asterisk indicates a fireplace, and a complete absence of asterisks indicates that the inventory does not show whether the rooms had fireplaces. Many inventories do not provide information about rooms at all. Valuations from inventories given here relate to household goods and do not include debts, leases and cash in hand; the value of farming or other working stock is given separately if substantial; values are to the nearest pound. Rents are given where known. The initials in brackets at the end indicate the landholder in 1665 (see Appendix 1).

The directory

No.	Name	Tax status	H	Occupation	Status etc.	Location
						Lower Richmond Road, from Lower Common to the High Street
1	Deliverance Smith	ex	4	Bricklayer 1662; gardener 1668. (Note 1)	Ale 1669, OP 1673. Pew. <C>	Messuage and Starkey's Close, used as a garden, N of the Putney-Barnes highway, 1666 (2 ½ acres on 1636 map). Rent £10 pa 1670. (JP)
2	Jonathan Whitehorne	ex	2	4	<P>	
3	Thomas Halland	poore	2		<P*>	
4	Symon Foord	poore+	2		<P>	
5	George Gearks [Jux]	noe entr	6	Gardener. (Note 2)	OP 1679. Pew. Lit. Aged 42. <C>	
6	Walter Sisum [junior]	ex	1	Gardener.	<P>	
7	William Bemish	ex	2	Gardener. (Note 3)	Side 1656-8, SH 1661, OP 1665-6, Head 1679. Pew. Lit. (Vestryman 1684.) <C>	

8	Mr [Thomas] Davis	ex	8	Citizen & goldsmith of London (1674).[5]	Vestryman. CW 1663-4. Pew. <R>	Between Costrell (No. 9) and Thomas Davis in 1662 was William Milborne, 3 hearths, which was one of 4 leased with Thomas Davis's and Thomas Millar's, the lease to start in 1668; in 1670 the lease also covered land late occupied by John Costrell. Total rent of the 4 messuages 1668 £24 pa. Probably part of the present Winchester House. (DW)
8A	*Thomas Millar*	*poor*	*1*	Gardener 1653.	<P*>	One of the 4 messuages including No. 8. (DW)
9	John Costrell	poore*	*2*	Victualler.	Plague 1. <P>	Leased cottage and garden from William Wymondsold 1651 (£6 pa); a Wymondsold tenant 1670. Probably the predecessor of the present Duke's Head (Note 4). (DW)
10	Lewis Ashfeild	ex	2	Waterman.	Ale 1654. Illit. Aged 51. <P>	
11	Martha How-man [Matthew Homan]	poore +	2	Waterman	Aged 29. <P*>	
12	Mr [John] Davis	noe entr	—		<C>	
13	Lady Rose [Anne Ruse]	noe entr	9		Pew. <R>	Lease of 1653 from William Wymondsold; rent £14 pa. (DW)
14	Winnafull Morrill	noe entr	6		<C>	
15	Mr Thomas Bryan [Bryant]	ex	8	Boatman/ waterman.	SH 1664. <C>	
16	Mr [Mrs Isabel] Pennington	ex	7		Pew. <R>	
17	Mr [Henry] Portman	ex	18	(Master of school for girls.)[6]	Vestryman. CW 1644-7, Con 1651, SH 1656, CW 1676. Pew. Aged 55. <R>	House known as the Barber's Apron. Portman was a Wymondsold tenant 1672. Apparently the property held under a lease of 1650 for £50 pa. (DW)
18	Mr Noah Bridges	ex	10	(Master of school for boys.)[7]	Vestryman. CW 1653-4/60. Pew. Aged 52. <R>	
19	Richard Higgenburrowe [Higginbottom]	poore * +	2	Tailor.I	Side 1671-3, OP 1677, Side 1680-93. Pew. Plague 4. <C>	
20	Daniell Constant	poore+	2	(Waterman 1681.) Owns a boat 1681.[8]	Ale 1665, Head 1667, Side 1671-3, OP 1678. Pew. Widow owned a Putney alehouse 1683. <C>	Inventories 1681 & 1683: kitchen*, chamber up 1 pair of stairs*, garrett; £16 & £18.[9]

20A	*Robert Coombes*		*4*	Waterman.	Side 1633-4, OP 1643-5, Con 1644, SH 1646/54. Small landholder. Illit. Plague 2. Aged 72. <C>	One of William Webb's 7 tenements (one possibly N of the road), 1664/5. The order varies in the two entries. Combes's house was adjacent to Webb's wharf. Inventory 1683: £4.[10] (WW)
21	Mr Webes [William Webb]	empty	4	Citizen & merchant tail-or of London.	Pew. <C>	Evidently one of Webb's 7 tenements (possibly Combes's - No. 20A - if Combes was temporarily absent). (WW)
22	Edward Cooke	ex	2	Ship carpenter.	Head 1662, OP 1668, Con 1672. Lit. <C>	One of Webb's 7 tenements, 1664/5. (WW).
23	Mr Webelan [Webb?]	empty	2			Presumably one of Webb's 7 tenements. (WW)
23A	*George Dollard*			Waterman.	Plague 2. <P>	One of Webb's 7 tenements, 1664/5; this and the next 2 are in the order given in 1665. (WW)
23B	*Hugh Harwood*			Waterman.	OP 1682. Plague 1. <P?>	As No. 23A, 1664/5. (WW)
23C	*John Rogers*	*poor*	*1*		Casual poor relief 1665/6. <P*>	As No. 23A, 1665. (WW)
24	Capt [John] Blunt	noe entr	*13*	Captain; gentleman.[11]	Vestryman. Small landholder in Roehampton. <R>	Capital messuage, 1666 (Blunt not mentioned). Mansion of which the surviving part was later known as Clyde House. (JY)
25	Edward Crostid	poore	2	Waterman. I	Aged 35. <P*>	Probably one of 4 tenements near the E part of No. 24, 1666/73 (Crosted mentioned only in 1673). One of these (N of the road) was later the Three Tuns, which became the Eight Bells. (MC)
26	Margarett Haughton	not quite built	3		<C>	As No. 25, 1666; brick tenement built on E part of the wharf.[12] (MC)
27	John Purser	ex	2	Waterman. I	<P>	As No. 25, 1666/73.[13]
28	John Crowcher [Crucher]	poore *+	2	Waterman. I	Pew. <C?>	One of 2 messuages opposite churchyard and ferry place, 1685. (DW)
29	[Susanna] Cook widd	noe d.	4	Widow of waterman.	Plague 2. <C>	Part of 2 cottages and a brandy shop near the Red Lion, occupied by John Cooke, 1685. Inventory of William Cooke 1662: low room [kitchen]*, next low room*, cellar, 'the chamber over Simonds house', next chamber, third chamber, garretts, sheds in yard; £34.[14] (DW).
30	— [Hester] Symones jun widd	ex	2	Butcher.	Held property in Morden.[15] Plague 4. <C>	Inventory of Stephen Symonds 1664: £5; of Hester Symonds 1666: £9 (part only).[16]

						High Street, west side, from Red Lion south to Felsham Road
31	Andrew Willowe [Weller]	empty	12	Vintner; (innholder).	Vestryman. Side 1653-4, OP 1661, Con 1664, SH 1669. Lit. <C>	Inn called the Red Lion. Leased by Francis Clarke from William Wymondsold 1649 for £24 pa. (DW)
32	Thomas Kitt [Kite]	exanc-itur	12	(Innholder.)	Vestryman. Head 1646, Con 1650, SH 1655, Side 1659, SC 1677-8. Pew. Illit. Plague 1. <C>	Inn called the White Lion. Inventory of Thomas Lister 1673: Moon*, Star*, Sun, King's Head*, Queen's Head, store house, Castle*, Crown*, Lion*, Rose*, widow's room, wash house, Bull Head*, kitchen*, wine cellar, beer cellar; £105.[17] (DW)
33	Mr [Edward] Rogers	empty	10	Innholder.	Vestryman. OP 1644-6, Con 1648, SH 1653, CW 1656-8, OP 1670. Pew. <C>	Inn called the Bull, 1666. Rent (Ann Rogers) £20 pa 1670. Rebuilt c.1630.[18] (JP)
34	James Russell	ex	3	(Victualler.)	OP 1672, Side 1674-7, Con 1678. Pew. Illit. <C>	One of 3 tenements abutting N on Pettiward, S on George Platt, W on Mrs Palmer, 1685. Russell's trade token of 1667 says 'at the Falcon in Putney' (the Falcon is named in the manorial survey of 1617). Inventory 1688: garretts, coffee room, 2 rooms backwards, kitchen, buttery, room backwards, room next the street, wash-house, shed; £14 + £10 stock.[19] (DW)
35	William Compe [Kemp]	poore*	1	Chandler.	<P>	
36	Mary Markes [Marquis]	noe entr	6	Widow of victualler.	Plague 4. <C>	Her husband's trade token of 1660 showed a wheatsheaf (the arms of the Earl of Exeter - the alehouse was known as the Lord of Exeters Arms in 1617). By 1726 it was formerly the Wheatsheaf.[20]
37	— [Dorothy] Burges widd	noe entr	6	Widow of baker.	Pew. <C>	Leased by Daniel Burges from William Wymondsold 1655 (£10 pa). Inventory of Daniel Burges 1662: hall*, great chamber*, middle chamber*, 'june chamber', stable; £30.[21] (DW)
37A	*William Butterfeild*		*1*	Waterman; manorial bailiff 1665.[22]	Plague 3. Aged 28. <P>	Listed about here in 1664 list, though the order changes (to Kemp, Marquis, Butterfield, Dunstall, Burges, Jackson), perhaps indicating that there were larger houses facing the street and smaller ones behind.
38	John Fathrey [Fawdrie]	poore [23]	2	Waterman 1682. Had a horse 1666.[24]	Side 1646-7. <P>	Lease of 1654 from William Wymondsold (£12 pa). (DW)
39	Richard Dun-stan [Tunstall]	poore*	2	Waterman.	Plague 1. <P>	

40	Robert Jackson	poore *+	2	Tallow chandler.	Side 1664, Con 1665, SH 1668. Pew. <C>	One of the tenements formed from the former Queen's Arms (3 occupants listed in 1664). Whole tenement worth £18 pa 1657.[25] (GP)
41	Robert Cooke	ex	3		Head 1663. Plague 3. <C>	As No. 40. (GP)
42	John Pilkington	empty	2	Coachman.	Ale 1667. Pew. <C?>	Pilkington was described as an 'inmate' in Burnham's house in 1662.[26]
43	Henry Barnham [Burnham]	ex	3	Cooper.	Ale 1648, OP 1659, Con 1677. Pew. Aged 50. <C>	As No. 40. (GP).
44	William Younge	<u>poore</u>	2	Basketmaker. I	Ale 1662. Plague 6. <P*>	Inventory 1665: £7.[27]
45	Symon Morgan [Mowden]	poore	1	Waterman.	Casual poor relief to his wife 1665/6 'in her lying in & husbands absence at sea'. Plague 2. <P*>	
46	Thomas Chare	poore *+	1	Waterman.I	Pew. Plague 2. <P>	One of 8 dwellings, 1669. (HH)
47	Mr Hubard	poore	2			('Mr Hubard' is perhaps a reference to the landlord.)
48	John Carpenter	empty	2	Waterman.I	Ale 1661, Head 1664, Con 1683. Pew. Illit. Twice press-ganged in the 1650s.[28] <C>	As No. 46. (HH)
49	Phillipp Howard	poore *+	2	Waterman.I	Plague 4. <P>	
50	John Wright	poore *+	2	Waterman.I	Ale 1657, Head 1661. Pew. <C>	As No. 46. (HH)
50A	Thomas Sayers [Seers]		*1*	Waterman.	Plague 2. <P>	As No. 46; listed between Cordwell Hammond and Charles Hubbert (with 1 other small house) in 1668 rate, and between Hubbert and John Wright in 1669; probably at the entrance to the alley. (HH)
51	Mrs Hubard [Jane Hubbert]	ex	14	Widow of gentleman.[29]	<R>	As No. 46. (Occupied by the Earl of Nottingham 1674.) (HH)
52	Cordwell Hamon [Hammond]	ex	9	Citizen & draper of London.[30]	Vestryman. Con 1663, CW 1664-5. Pew. Aged 35. <R>	One of 11 tenements (including the 8 starting at No. 55), 1664. Inventory 1681: first garrett, man's garrett, blue, best, middle & green chambers, parlour, hall, banqueting house [in garden], kitchen, yard, cellar, wash-house.[31] (DC)
53	one	empty	7			(DC)

54	John Hinton [Hingeston]	ex	7	Court musician.[32]	Pew. Illit. <R>	As No. 52. (DC)
55	Thomas Jury [Juer]	poore *+	2	Baker 1651; waterman 1674.[33]	OP & Head 1647, Side 1650. Small landholder. Pew. Aged 78. <C>	One of 8 small cottages 1664/9, abutting S on the way to Roehampton, E on the said way, N on Conyers. Inventory of widow Joan Juer 1678: kitchen*, shop, chamber over shop, her lodging chamber, garrett over chamber; £13.[34] (DC)
55A	*John Char*		*1*	Waterman.	<P>	As No. 55; listed between Juer and Emberton in 1664/9. (DC)
56	James Eborton [Emberton]	ex	2	Blacksmith.I	Side 1633, Head 1648, Side 1663, Head 1665, Side 1667-8.[35] Pew. Illit. <C>	As No. 55. Later recorded as 3 hearths, one a forge.[36] Inventory 1682: kitchen*, little room, chamber over kitchen, other chamber*, next chamber, cellar, shop ('working tooles & some old iron'); £8.[37] (DC)
57	John Braynon [Bryan]	poore[38]	2	Waterman.[39]I	Illit. <P*>	As No. 55. (DC)
58	Henry Francombe [Franckham]	noe entr	2	Waterman.I	<P>	As No. 55. (DC)
59	— Horton [Mary Holton] widd	poore	2	Widow of waterman.	Casual poor relief 1665-6. <P*>	As No. 55. (DC)
59A	*Widd [Anne] Selbey*	*poor*	*2*	Widow of drayman.I	Casual poor relief 1657/8, 1665/6. <P*>	As No. 55; listed last in 1664 (with one other dwelling after Holton).[40] (DC)
						In the fields west of the High Street
60	Thomas Lowe [Law]	cx[41] [poor 1664]	2	Waterman 1653/74.[42]	Ale 1656. <P>	Tenement with 1 rood in Caddow Shott, abutting E on Dawes Wymondsold, S on Worple Way, 1674. (MS)
61	John Martin	empty	3	Husbandman and victualler (unlicensed).[43]	SH 1651, Head 1652, OP 1679. Pew. Illit. <C>	In 1662 Martin was listed with 3 hearths between Deliverance Smith and William Bemish (Nos. 1 & 7 in 1665), and he was probably on the S side of Lower Richmond Road. There was a tenement lately built there S of Starkey's Close in 1658, then occupied by John Hales, gardener (perhaps the predecessor of the Half Moon).
62	Dorothy Beary	poore	2		<P*>	
63	Richard Forrester [Foster]	noe d.	6	Waterman. (Note 5)	Head 1645, OP 1656-8, SH 1664, Con 1670, SC 1672-6. Pew. <C>	The second strip westwards from Walkers Place in Stony or Gravel Shot was stated in the early 1660s to be 'near his [Foster's] new house westward'.[44]
64	Peter Rogers	poore *+	2	Gardener/ labourer.	Side 1648, Ale 1650, Head 1651, OP 1654-5, Con 1661. Pew. Illit. <C>	Tenement on John Young's land, 1666. (i.e. land between No. 24 and Felsham Road.) (JY)

65	Thomas Howell [junior]	poore+	2	Waterman.	Casual poor relief to wife in her husband's absence at sea 1665/6.[45] <P*>	
66	Joseph Smyth	poore	1	Gardener.I	Casual poor relief 1665-6. Lit. Plague 2. <P*>	Smith's rent was paid to Carter in 1665, and the Carters held what had been Mathias Smyth's plot in Stony Shot, which later contained many small dwellings.[46]
67	Thomas Bale [Ball]	poore+	2	(Husband-man.) Had 2 horses, 3 pigs and barley and wheat in 1681.	SH 1671, Head 1674, OP 1676. Pew. <C>	Probably the newly-built messuage with barns in the middle of 4 acres in Long Furlong, adjoining the way to Putney church, occupied by Ball's widow, Suzanne in 1685 (the site until recently of the Quill), as Ball's position in the 1668 rate suggests. Inventory 1681: kitchen, room over kitchen, buttery, little room, cellar, barn, stable; £9 + farming £25.[47] (JW)
68	Mr Rackes [William Ridges]	empty	4		Former London Alderman.[48] Vestryman. Pew. <R>	One of 3 tenements with 40 rods of land abutting S [N] on the lane from Putney Street to the common fields and N [S?] on Thomas Maund, 1663 (only Christopher Nash listed as occupant). (HN)
69	William Fisher	ex	1	Waterman.	Ale 1651, OP & Head 1653. Pew. Plague 2. <C>	
70	Francis Fisher	noe d. [poor 1664]	2	Bricklayer.[49]	Pew. <P?>	Abuts the lane from Putney town into the fields, between the tenements of Edward Tillyer E and Alderman Rydges [W], 1658. Rent £2½ pa 1669. (JP)
71	— Drowe widd	<u>poore</u>	2	Widow of waterman/ labourer.	Casual poor relief 1665-6. <P*>	
72	John Cane	poore*	1	Gardener.	<P>	
						Along the west side of the High Street, from Felsham Road south to Upper Richmond Road
73	Edward Tiller [Tillyer]	poore*	2	(Victualler.)I	<P>	Tenement known as the Five Bells, adjoining No. 74, 1658. Rent £5½ pa 1670. (JP)
74	Richard Grimes	ex	4	Waterman; (victualler).	Ale 1647/9, Side 1653-4, Head 1657, OP 1660, Con 1669. Pew. <C>	Tenement known as the Blue Anchor, 1658. Rent £11 pa 1669. Inventory 1681: £5.[50] (JP)
75	— Sellus widd [probably Mary Silley]	<u>poore</u>	1	Widow of waterman.	Casual poor relief 1665/6. Plague 2. <P*>	(3 tenements occupied by Beyner/Penn/Owen, abutting S & W on Thomas Juer, N on Pettiward, E on Putney Street, 1673. (TM))
76	Mr Mane	empty	2		<P>	

77	John Mascall	ex	5	Poulterer.	Pew. (Vestryman 1684.) <C>	Tenement, 1647. (TJ)
78	Edward Mathas [Matthews]	poore+	2	Waterman.	Wife Margery accused of being 'a common night walker' 1664.[51] <P*>	(Between Mascall, No. 77, and Mowden, No. 84, in the 1668 rate were just 2 names, one of which, William Goodyard or Gudchere, lived in Pepper Alley in 1679. Rent for one of the houses £1.10s.0d. pa 1673.)[52] (TJ)
79	Richard Iremonger [Ironmonger]	empty	2		Plague 1. <P>	
80	Rowland Jones	poore	2		<P*>	
81	Edward Jones	ex	3	Blacksmith/ locksmith.I	Ale 1666. <C>	
82	Robert Cauten [Cuerton]	poore*	2	Waterman.	Head 1651, OP 1652, SH 1653. <C>	Tenement W of Putney Street, adjoining No. 83, 1658. (JP)
83	— Sauier widdowe	poore	2		<P>	Tenement with barn W of Putney Street between tenements occupied by Thomas Jewer, John Mowden and Robert Cuerton, occupied by Stephen Symonds 1658. (JP)
84	John Mauden [Mowden]	ex	5	Cooper; victualler.I	Con 1647, SH 1651, Side 1665-6. Pew. Lit. Aged 65. <C>	Tenement W of Putney Street, abutting W on Worple Way, S on Doe's tenement, N on Stephen Symonds' tenement, 1658. Rent £6 pa 1669. Evidently the Coopers' Arms alehouse. (JP)
85	William Drowe [Doe]	empty	3	Baker.	OP 1652, Head 1654. <C>	Tenement, bakehouse and 2 barns, W of Putney Street, adjoining No. 86, 1658. Rent £20 pa 1670. (JP)
86	— Hared widowe [Frances Harwood]	noe d.	3		<C>	Tenement W of Putney Street abutting S on farmhouse of William Powell, N on William Doe's tenement, 1658. (JP)
87	Nicholas Maide [Meade]	ex	2	Carpenter.	Ale 1657, Head 1658, Side 1660-1, OP 1667, SH 1669, Con 1675. Pew. <C>	6 tenements held by Nicholas Meades 1685, abutting W, S & N on Pettiward and part of the Worple and E on the High Street. (WP)
88	Robert [Roger] Andrews	ex	2		Head 1666, OP 1671, Side 1674-6, Con 1676, OP 1682. <C>	
89	Richard Clarke	poore*	2	Waterman.	<P>	
90	Henry Williams	poore*	2	Waterman.I	<P>	
91	Richard Crowe [Crane]	ex	2	Bricklayer.	Ale 1664, Side 1669-70, Head 1672. Small landholder. Pew. Illit. Plague 4. Aged 28. <C>	

92	Richard Peeve [Penn]	poore *+	2	Waterman.	Ale 1664, Head 1677. Pew. Aged 38. <C>	
93	Richard Vauhanne	poore+	2	Tailor.	<P*>	One of 10 tenements between tenements of Gainsford on S and of Powell on N, abutting E on the street and W on Glasinghall, 1658.[53] (JP)
94	— [Ellen] Eldridge widdowe	poore	1	Widow of waterman. I (Kept by a servant 1672.)[54]	<P*>	As No. 93. (JP)
95	Thomas Denninge	ex	2	Carpenter; (rent collector).[55]	Vestryman. Head 1652, OP 1655-6, Side 1660, SH 1663. Small landholder. Pew. Aged 40. <C>	As No. 93. (JP)
96	John Maskill [Mascall] sen.	noe d.	3	Poulterer.	Head 1656, OP 1659, SH 1663, Con 1667, SC 1669-71. Small landowner. <C>	
97	widd Foord [Jane Forth]	poore	1		Plague 1. <P*>	Rent of £1 paid to Thomas Denning 1652-3, but not clear whether for a year.[56]
98	Thomas Ellitts [Elliot]	poore	2	Shoemaker.	<P*>	As No. 93. (JP)
99	John Symonds	ex	2	Butcher.	Side 1669-70, Con 1674. Pew. Illit. <C>	Inventory 1676: £11.[57]
100	James Townes [Chownes]	poore *+	2	Cordwainer 1700.	Head 1656. <C?>	
101	Joseph Wardners	dead	2			
102	Miles Searse	poore+	2	I	<P>	
103	William Chare	poore *+	2	Waterman. I	Con 1688, OP 1694. Pew. <C?>	
104	William Holton	poore	1	Waterman.	<P*>	
105	Richard Sefey [Keffey][58]	poore	1	Waterman/ labourer. I	Casual poor relief 1665/6. Plague 1. <P*>	

106	Richard Fisher	noe entr	6	Carpenter; victualler 1678.I	Ale 1644-6, OP 1657-8, Con 1662, Side 1664-5, SH 1670. Small landholder. Pew. Lit. <C>	Hester Gainsford was licensed in 1674 to lease out a tenement occupied by Richard Fisher and John Hill; in 1678 Fisher's tenement was the White Hart, and the 2 abutted E on Putney Street, S on a tenement of Wymondsold and N & W on Pettiward. Fisher's trade token of c.1660 said 'at ye White Hart in Putney'. Inventory 1679: kitchen*, parlour*, chamber over parlour*, lodging chamber*, passage room; £42.[59] (HG)
107	Richard Fisher	empty	2			
108	Mr Wimorsoles [Wymondsold]	empty	12			(DW)
109	Edward Slaughter [Sclater]	noe d.	6	Minister of Putney.	Vestryman. Aged 42. <C>	One of 4 messuages in the middle of the W side of the street abutting S on Pettiward, N on Hester Gainsford, 1685. (DW)
110	Robert Hobbes	<u>poore</u>	2	Dyer.	Soldier in parliamentary army 1655. <P*>	
111	Alexander Howell	poore *+	2	Waterman.I	Ale 1665. Pew. <C?>	
112	George Biddle [Beadle]	poore *+	2	Waterman 1678.	Head 1665, OP 1673. <C>	Tenement W of Putney Street between tenements of Richard Nicholls and Thomas Kentish, 1658. (Nos. 112 to 120 appear to be in order, S to N, in the list of property inherited by Pettiward in 1658.) Rent £3½ pa 1670. (JP)
113	— widdowe Nicholls	<u>poore</u>	3	Widow of bricklayer. (Victualler?)	Casual poor relief 1668; pension by 1674. <P*>	Tenement called White Hart W of Putney Street (occupied by Richard Nicholls), 1658. Rent £3 pa 1669. (JP)
114	Robert White	ex	2		<P>	
115	Clime Chomes [Clement Chownes]	poore	2		<P*>	One of 3 tenements W of Putney Street occupied by Christopher Miller, widow Kyng & Clement Chownes, 1658. (JP)
116	Alderman Petti-well [Pettiward, landlord]	empty	2			(JP)
117	John Hey [Hayes]	noe d.	2	Poulterer. (Note 6)	SH 1665-6, OP 1674. Pew. <C>	
118	Christopher Milles [Miller]	poore*	2	Gardener.[60]	<P>	As No. 115.
119	Widd Hose [Margaret Hayes]	poore*	1	Poulterer.	<P?>	Tenement with barn, between tenement of Christopher Miller S [sic] and widow King N, 1658. (JP)

120	Francis Button	ex	2	Husbandman.[61] I (Held 5½ acres of Pettiward land 1688.)	SH 1659-60, OP 1675. Illit. <C>	By its placing in the 1658 list, tenement with barn W of Putney Street, abutting N & W on premises of Wymondsold, S [sic] on cottage of Christopher Miller, E on the highway (N & S clearly reversed).[62] Rent £7 pa 1669. (JP)
121	Mr John Turner	ex	14	Merchant.	Vestryman. CW 1659-60. Pew. <R>	One of 3 large houses on the present sites of Norroy and Chelverton Roads and the railway. Turner's was the northernmost, and was a 'newbuilt bricke howse' in 1655, between premises occupied by Mrs Yardley S and Henry White N; with 2 closes totalling 9 acres. Rent £21 pa from 1655, plus £160 fine.[63] (DW)
122	Mr Early [Mrs Olive Yardley]	ex	9	Sister of Clerk of Privy Council under Charles I.[64]	<R>	As No. 121. Olive Yardley leased a messuage and garden from William Wymondsold 1650 (£14 pa). Inventory of her son William Salmon 1680: Note 7. (DW)
123	Mr Francis Clarke	empty	11	Merchant.[65]	London Alderman 1666; knighted May 1665. Vestry-man. CW 1666-7. Pew. Aged 43. <R>	As No. 121. Had 6 acre close, 1674. Leased messuage and close from William Wymondsold 1654 (£25 pa). (DW)
						Up the west side of Putney Hill to the windmill and back along the east side of Putney Hill
124	George Giles	exam-inatur [poore 1664][66]	3	Victualler. (Note 8)	Head 1650, SH 1671. <C>	Probably one of 4 tenements just W of the foot of the Hill recorded in 1617 and shown on the 1636 map, including the Anchor. Lease of 1650 from William Wymondsold (£4 pa). The Anchor's successor is now the Fox.
125	Kinge widdowe	poore	3		<P*>	As No. 124.
126	— Roseman widd [Jane Bosman]	poore+[67]	2		<P>	As No. 124.
127	Thomas Mab-dene [Mabsden]	poore*	3	Wheelwright. I	<C>	As No. 124.
128	Francis Juse	poore*	1		<P>	
129	Weymorsum [Wymondsold] Justice	empty	—			
129A	*Thomas Silley*		*1*	Husbandman.	Plague 1. <P>	Possibly in Upper Richmond Road W of Putney Hill; listed 3rd after No. 132 and before No. 137 in 1664 list; after No. 124 and Putney Park House in 1668 rate.
129B	*Mr John Robins*		*12*		<R>	Putney Park.[68]

130	Henry Crane	ex	4	(Husbandman 1679.) (Note 9)	Ale 1662, SH 1667-8. Pew. <C>	Directly after John Sergeant (No. 139) in the 1662 list, when the collector passed up the Hill alternating from side to side. Widow Crane was occupying a messuage with 3 acres in the SW quadrant of Putney in 1685. Inventory 1679: kitchen*, room by kitchen*, chamber over kitchen*, other chamber*; £13 + farming £221.[69] Leased messuage and land from William Wymondsold 1662 (£14 pa). (DW)
131	John Smith	ex	1		<P>	'at ye Comon gate' 1671 (register).
132	John Anderton	ex	4	Husbandman/ labourer. I	<C>	'at the Common gate' 1667 (register). An Anderton was occupying a messuage with 2 acres near the White Hart somewhere in the SW quadrant of Putney in 1685. Leased 2 cottages from William Wymondsold 1660 (£12 pa). (DW)
132A	*John Bell*	*poor*	*1*	Labourer.	Casual poor relief 1665/6. Aged 86; born in Putney. <P*>	Licensed to hold 3 rods and a cottage on Putney Common in his own occupation, Dec 1666; in the list of exempt in 1664, between Nos. 125 and 133, adjacent to No. 133. (MW)
133	Andrewe Driver	poore	2	Innholder/ victualler. I Pension as maimed soldier, 1663; manorial bailiff 1665.[70]	Lit. Aged 40. <P*>	Possibly the White Hart, near the South Heath Gate, mentioned in 1629.[71]
133A	*Widd Cutt*	*poor*	*1*	I	Casual poor relief 1665/6. <P*>	'at ye coman gate' 1665 (register); between Driver and Mathews in the list of exempt in 1664.
134	Widd Mathas [William Mathews]	poore	2	Husbandman.[72] I	<P*>	'in ye common' 1663. Licensed to hold 40 rods of common land and a cottage on it in his own occupation, 1666. Only 1 hearth 1664. (MW)
135	Burne widdowe	poore	2		<P*>	
136	Robert White	empty	10	(Victualler.)	Ale 1650, OP 1663. <C>	At the mill 1663 (register). Leased messuage and alley (for bowling) from William Wymondsold 1659 (£24 pa).
137	Robert Milles [Miles]	poore*	2	Victualler (unlicensed).[73]	<P>	'att mill' in 1664 list.
138	John Buller [Butler]	poore*	1	Husbandman.	Head 1641. Casual poor relief 1666-7; parish pension by 1674. <P*>	The order in the 1662 list, when the collector went up the Hill alternating from side to side, suggests that Butler was at the top of the Hill, and the order in 1665 indicates the E side. Sir John Lawrence paid Butler's 'chimney money' in 1685-6.[74]

139	John Sergeant	ex	4	Husbandman (farmed 50 acres N of Putney Heath 1685).I	OP 1665-6. Pew. <C>	Probably one of the buildings E of Putney Hill shown on the 1636 map.
140	Capt Lingelove [Jonah Lindloffe]	noe d.	4		<C>	As No. 139.
141	Sr John Lawrence of London	exatur	31	Merchant (worth £2000 pa 1660).[75]	Lord Mayor of London 1664-5. Vestryman. Landholder in Putney. <R>	House known as Coalecroft[76] or (in the 18th century) Lime Grove. With 85 acres, 1656. Inventories 1655 & 1692: Notes 10 and 11. (JL)
						High Street, east side, from Upper Richmond Road northwards to Putney Bridge Road
142	Mr Wymersum [Dawes Wymondsold]	ex	37	(Gentleman.)	Sheriff of Surrey 1666. Vestryman. CW 1665-6. Landholder in Putney. <R>	House on site of present Putney Station, built 1635-6.[77] With 2 closes totalling 12½ acres. Inventory 1675: Note 12. (DW)
143	Sr Richard Ford [His son-in-law, Peter Proby, in 1661-74 except 1665]	empty	12	Merchant.[78]	London Alderman; Lord Mayor of London 1670; MP. Aged 52. (Proby was Vestryman; CW 1668-9 & 1680-1.) <R>	House on site of present Disraeli Road, later known as Grove House. Leased by Peter Proby from William Wymondsold 1661 (£30 pa). Inventory of Peter Proby 1684: Note 13. (DW)
144	Sr Thomas Chamberlayne	empty	*16*	Merchant.[79]	Vestryman. CW 1654-5. Property in London, Putney, Beds and Suffolk. Governor of East India Company 1662-3.[80] Aged 66. <R>	The White House, with 1½ acres, abutting W on Putney Street, S on Proby's garden, N & E on Warren's garden,1670. Later known as Essex House. (TC)
145	Mr Nicholas Warren	exatur	11	Merchant.	Vestryman. CW 1667-8. Pew. Aged 41. <R>	House on site of present Werter Road. Lease of messuage etc. from William Wymondsold 1654 (£20 pa). (DW)
146	William Humfrys	poore+[81]	2	Waterman.I	Head 1641. Pew. Illit. <C?>	Associated with No. 145. (DW)
147	Alderman [John] Pettiward	ex	*20*	Merchant; ironmonger.[82]	London Alderman. Vestryman. CW 1661. Landowner in Putney and Suffolk. Pew. <R>	House later (partly rebuilt) known as Fairfax House, 1658/72. Inventory (of Roger Pettiward) 1675: Note 14. (JP)
148	Mr Roberts	empty	9		<R>	The parsonage (held by the tithe owner).
149	Anthony Mar... [Marrant]	noe d.	3	Blacksmith/ farrier.	Ale 1663, Head 1669. <C>	

150	Mr Pooreman	empty	7		<C>	
151	Mrs [Mary] Norman	exatur	2		Small landholder. Pew. <C>	One of 3 tenements or cottages, abutting N on John Pettiward's house & land, S on parsonage & yard, W on the highway, 1673. (MN)
152	Capt Frogmorton [William Throckmorten]	empty	11	Merchant.[83]	Vestryman. CW 1669-70. Pew. Aged 49. <R>	Formerly the Campions' mansion, later known as Cromwell House. Leased by Throckmorten for £33 pa 1664.[84] (JP)
						East along Putney Bridge Road to the common sewer and back along the riverside and Brewhouse Lane
153	Walter Sysom [Sisam]	exatur	4	Gardener. (Note 15)	Vestryman. OP 1650-1, Side 1655, CW 1661-2. Small landholder. Pew. Lit. <C>	Tenement with 3 acres, 1646; associated with Campion's mansion;[85] tenement & 2 acres abutting W on Henry White, E on William Garrett, N on way from Putney to Wandsworth, S on William Wymondsold (no occupier given), 1658. Leased by Sisam for £10 pa 1644;[86] rent £15 pa 1669. (JP)
154	Richard White	poore	1		<P*>	The premises (inc. Campion's mansion and Sisam's) mortgaged by Campion to Henry White 1646 included 2 tenements and a barn, but these are not mentioned 1658. (JP)
155	Nicholas Smith	exatur [poor 1664]	3	Victualler (unlicensed);[87] brewer.	Head 1668, OP 1675, Con 1679, SC 1685/8/93. Pew. Illit. <C>	
156	William Garrett	poore*	2	Waterman. (Note 16)	Head 1640, SH 1659. Small landholder. Pew. Plague 1. <C>	Garrett held one acre on which houses had been built, 1666. His new building was encroaching on the Putney-Wandsworth road in 1642. 3 dwellings on this site in 1700. (WG)
157	Thomas Garratt	gone	2	Waterman.[88] (Had 1 cow, 1 hog and a boat in 1699.)	Ale 1666, Side 1667-8, SC 1669, Head 1670, OP 1676, SC 1677-9/81-4, Con 1684, SC 1688/93, CW 1692-3. Pew. Lit. Aged 31. (Vestryman 1687.) <C>	Inventory 1699: chamber*, chamber, kitchen*, wash-house; £14.[89]
158	Almeshouses		12			Almshouses built by Sir Abraham Dawes by 1636; brick-built, with courtyard N, pump yard W and 'twelve devided gardens southward to the twelve devided rooms'.[90] The rebuilt almshouses still stand in Putney Bridge Road.

159	— [Elizabeth] Hunt widdow	noe d.	4	Widow of gardener.[91]	<C>	Messuage with large garden beyond the almshouses, with 13 acres, 1685. Probably the messuage and garden leased by Francis Hunt from William Wymondsold 1651 (£15 pa). The house may still exist. (DW)
160	John Leeay [Lee]	exatur	4	Wharfinger; victualler.I	Ale 1667, Head 1669. Pew. <C>	Of Putney Gutter 1661;[92] at the wharf 1661 (register). Lee's halfpenny token of 1668 showed an anchor, but also 3 tuns. (ST)
161	Forrow [Pharoah] Clarke	<u>poore</u>	2	Bargeman.I [93]	<P*>	
162	Nane Silley	<u>poore</u>	1	Widow of husbandman.	Casual poor relief 1668. <P*>	Probably one of 4 small cottages at the E end of Putney near the dungwharf (one occupied by Anne's husband John Silley 1652). (ST)
163	William Belay [Bailey]	poore *+	2	Waterman.I	Ale 1644-5/61. Pew. <C?>	
164	Jeremy [Jeremiah] Jones	empty	3	Waterman. I	<P>	
165	William Saser	exatur	5		Pew. Aged 84. <C>	
166	John Cole	poore *+	3	Gardener. (Note 17)	Pew. <C>	Cole was responsible, with Terringham (his landlord) and John Lee, for repairing the footbridge over the sewer on the Putney-Wandsworth highway, and for keeping part of the sewer in repair, 1657.[94] (ST)
167	Sr William Tirringham [Terringham]	exatur	17	Knight of the Bath.[95]	Vestryman. <R>	Copt Hall. (ST)
168	Thomas Kentish	poore	2	Carpenter.[96]	Small landholder from 1665. Aged 32. <C>	Nos. 168-71 were apparently 4 tenements in Brewers Lane 1654/65, held by Stephen Smyth, one occupied by Thomas Howell. The northern part (presumably Nos. 168-70A), 67 by 48 feet, with buildings (not further described), was purchased by Thomas Kentish in May 1665, abutting (in 1706) S on the Putney-Wandsworth way, W on Brewers Lane, N on the tenement formerly of Anne Smith and E on a garden formerly Pettiward's. Site was until recently the Castle. (TK)
169	Thomas Howell [senior][97]	<u>poore</u>	2	Waterman.I	Parish pension from 1670. Plague 6. <P*>	As No. 168. (TK)
170	Edward Miller	<u>poore</u>	1	Waterman 1651/83.[98]	Ale 1651. <P*>	As No. 168. (TK)
170A	*Francis Fisher*		*2*	Brewer.	Pew. Illit. <P?>	One of Smyth's 4 dwellings, 1665; listed adjacent to widow Smith 1664. Inventory 1680: £4.[99]

171	— [Anne] Smith widd	poore*	2		<P>	Messuage in Brewers Lane, formerly Stephen Smyth's, 1670 (Anne was his mother, and obtained this as her widow's third, 1654). (SS)
172	Edward Smith	noe d.	2	Carpenter.[100]	Ale 1668. <P>	Small piece of land of 20 rods with tenement, 1656/60 (not occupied by Smith). (HN)
173	Richard Milles [Miles]	exatur	2	I	<P>	
174	Robert Tinder [Tindall]	poore	1	I	<P*>	
175	John Davis	poore+	2	Brewer's servant.	<P>	
176	Mr James White	empty	9	Brewer.	High Constable of Brixton Hundred 1663. SH 1655, OP 1663. Held land in 5 counties 1670.[101] Pew. Lit. <R>	Brewhouse and tenement (E of Brewhouse Lane), 1658/72. With 1 acre and 2 tenements. Rent £32½ pa 1669. (JP)
177	Mr Daniell Belte	exatur	10	Gentleman.[102]	CW 1672-3. Pew. Aged 50. <R>	Abuts E on premises of Terringham, W on the brewhouse, N on the Thames, S on the lower way from Putney to Wandsworth, 1658. With 4 acre close. (JP)
178	Thomas Howard [Harwood]	poore	2	Waterman 1633.I	Casual poor relief 1665-6. Plague 2. Aged 81. <P*>	
178A	*Allexander Baker*	*poor*	*2*	Waterman.I	Ale 1648. Casual poor relief 1665/6; pension from 1671.[103] <P*>	One of 4 tenements, 1663 (see No. 180). (DW)
179	Robert Last [Lawson]	poore *+	2	Waterman.I (Note 18)	Head 1673. Pew. Illit. Aged 43. <C>	As No. 178A; one of 2 tenements in Brewhouse Lane, 1685. (DW)
						From Putney Bridge Road north along the east side of the High Street
180	Edward Kinge	poore *+	2	Carpenter.	Ale 1656, Head 1658, Side 1661, OP 1664, Con 1666. Pew. Aged 36. <C>	One of 4 tenements abutting E [S] on way to Wandsworth by the stocks, N on premises of Huntley occupied by Oughton, W on High Street, E on Brewers Lane, 1663 (2 of the 4 apparently faced Brewhouse Lane; whole plot contained only a messuage & cottage 1651).[104] Inventory 1677: workhouse, cellar, kitchen*, parlour*, chambers over parlour and kitchen, 2 garretts; £21 + stock £15.[105] (DW)

181	Henry Driver	exatur	4	Victualler.	Head 1664, Con 1681. Pew. Lit. Plague 1. Aged 38. <C>	As No. 181. Inventory 1682: kitchen*, parlour*, little room by kitchen, chamber over kitchen, chamber over parlour*, back chamber; £19.[106] Rent £13 pa (1662 lease). Probably the later Queen's Head. (DW)
182	Mr John Outon [Oughton]	exatur	6	Gentleman 1643.	Vestryman. CW 1646-9. Pew. <R>	(RH)[107]
183	Robert Lowis [Lewis]	empty	6	Gentleman.	Vestryman. Ale 1663. Pew. <R>	One of 6 tenements and a barn, abutting E on Brewhouse Lane, N on widow Rogers, S on Wymondsold, 1688. New lease from Huntley, 1674. (RH)
184	Henry Tunstall	exatur	5	Glasier.	Vestryman. Ale 1652, OP 1653-4, Side 1655, Con 1658, CW 1662-3, SC 1670-1, CW 1685-6. Pew. Lit. Plague 1. Aged 39. <C>	As No. 183. Lease from Huntley, 1662. (RH)
185	Henry Tunstall	poore	2			
186	Edward Jure	poore *+	2	Waterman.I	Ale 1651/3. Inherited £20 pa from his father.[108] <P>	
187	John Kempe	poore *+	2	Chandler.	Head 1666, OP 1668, Con 1673, OP 1682, CW 1687-8. Pew. (Vestryman 1687.)[109] <C>	
188	Richard Brauten [Broughton]	noe d.	3	Waterman/ labourer.	Quaker 1665.[110] Lit. <P?>	Anne Rogers obtained 3 tenements 1663, to which 2 more had been added by 1668; Broughton mentioned 1668. Issued token showing the watermen's arms 1668.[111] (AR)
189	John East [senior]	exatur	2	Waterman.I	Pew. Aged 54. <C?>	As No. 188; East mentioned 1668. Inventory 1673: £8.[112] (AR)
190	Thomas Bannatt [Pannett]	exatur	3	Barber-surgeon.	OP 1667, SH 1670, CW 1677-8. Pew. <C>	As No. 188; Pannett mentioned 1663/5/8. Rooms in 1684: cellar with buttery therein, shop towards street, low room or kitchen backwards, chamber over shop, garrett over that chamber, chamber and garrett over kitchen, little closet to chamber over kitchen, house of easement adjoining stable, workhouse, wash-house, coal-house, stables and hayloft; garden 63 feet N-S (the entire width of Rogers' premises).[113] (AR)
191	Richard Cockes [Cox]	poore	3	Drayman.	<P*>	

192	Owen Cocke [Cooke]	poore *+	2	Shoemaker.	Head 1662, OP 1664, Con 1668/87. Pew. Lit. <C>	As No. 188; Cooke mentioned 1663/5/8. (AR)
193	William Cobbitt	empty	6	Butcher. (Note 19)	Con 1654, SH 1667. Pew. <C>	One of 3 tenements abutting S on Anne Rogers, W on royal way, N on churchyard, E on garden of John Dawes, 1667. Cobbett's premises included a slaughterhouse, 1656.[114] (DW)
194	Widdowe Coomes	poore	1	Widow of waterman.	Casual poor relief 1665-6; parish pension from 1668/9. <P*>	
195	Christopher Rogers	poore	2	Parish clerk (from 1663 to 1724).[115]	OP 1648; Head 1697. <P*>	As No.193.[116] (DW)
196	Mr [Henry] Portman	empty	11	(Had moved to No. 17.)		Church House, E of Putney Church. Capital messuage, with 3 tenements, 1657. Rent £20 pa 1644.[117] (JD)
197	Mr Jeremyah					
198	Edward Bon...	empty	7		<C>	
						Unlocated
P1	*Hugh Williams*	*poor*	*1*	Labourer.	Casual poor relief 1665/6. Plague 1. <P*>	One of 5 tenements in Pepper Alley, 1679, but probably elsewhere in 1665.
P2	*Hanry Vahon [Vaughan]*	*poor*	*2*	Tailor. (£3 pa for keeping the church clock and ringing the curfew bell from 1657). Had a horse 1665.[118]	Casual poor relief 1657/8, 1665/6; parish pension from 1668. <P*>	
P3	*Wid* [Mary] *Mager*	*poor*	*1*		Parish pension from 1668. <P*>	W side of High Street: between Nos. 71 and 78 in list of exempt in 1664; probably Pepper Alley.
P4	*Margery Jones*	*poor*	*1*		Casual poor relief 1665/6. Illit. <P*>	W side of High Street: immediately after No. 80 and before No. 93 in list of exempt in 1664.
P5	*Margery Deane*	*poor*	*2*	Widow of waterman.I	Casual poor relief 1665/6; parish pension 1670-3. <P*>	W side of High Street: next after Margery Jones in list of exempt in 1664.
P6	*Elizabeth Duffin*	*poor*	*1*		Casual poor relief 1665/6. <P*>	W side of High Street: next after Margery Deane in list of exempt in 1664.
P7	*Nicholas Kinge*	*poor*	*2*	Carpenter.	Pew. <P*>	W side of High Street: between Nos. 98 and 110 in list of exempt in 1664.

P8	*Sarah Randoll*	poor	*1*	Widow of waterman.	Illit. Pew. <P*>	Probably the Brewhouse Lane area, judging by her placing in the list of exempt in 1664.
P9	*Robert Millar*	poor	*2*	Gardener 1654/6; hus-bandman 1662; waterman 1662; labourer 1666.[119] (Note 20)	<P*>	Probably the dungwharf area, judging by his placing in the list of exempt in 1664.
						ROEHAMPTON
199	The Right Ho. Countess Devonshire	ex	57	Countess.	Landholder. <R>	Roehampton Great House (on site of present Grove House). With 350-acre park.[120]
200	William Harvey	ex	20		CW 1666/8. Landholder. <R>	House later known as Elm Grove (site now part of Roehampton University). With 14 acres, 1662. (WH)
201	George Jux lord		*2*	Gardener.	Ale 1650, Head 1651, Con 1654, Side 1655, OP 1658. <C>	Leased tenement and 6 acre Butchers Close (northernmost part of Elm Grove estate, W of Roehampton Lane, just S of present Fairacres) from the Harveys, 1654/62. 'Lord' may indicate it was sub-let. (WH)
202	Ralphe Dell	empty	2		Casual poor relief 1666 (if 'old Dell'). <P*>	(The Harvey premises included another tenement and 2 cottages, occupied by John Carter, 1654/62; the cottages may have been the encroachments on Roehampton Lane, recorded in 1617 and earlier.)[121]
203	Thomas Hewett	poore *+	1		Ale 1666. <P>	
204	John Farmer	empty	2		Ale 1646-7, Head 1654, Con 1667. Pew. <C>	Cottage on manorial waste, 1675. Possibly one of the 2 small cottages on land enclosed from Roehampton Lane long before. (MW)
205	Nicholas Beagent	ex	8	Baker.	Head 1641, Side 1643/6, Con 1647, SH 1650, OP 1656, Con 1661/5, OP 1668. <C>	Shared responsibility for scouring ditch from heath gate to Robert White's pales, 1656. But in 1676 occupied the tenement and 1 acre formerly Robert White's (see No. 207). Only 3 hearths 1664/74.

206	Nicholas Waxham	ex	3	Husbandman. (Note 21)	Vestryman. Side 1626, OP 1629/34, SH 1632/7, OP 1639, SH 1641, CW 1643, SH 1644-6, Side 1647-8, SH 1651, Con 1653, Side 1656-7, SH 1659, CW 1661, SH 1663 (see Note 21). Plague 1. Illit. <C>	Inventory 1666: £6 + farming £34.[122]
207	Mr Robert White	ex	6	Innholder. Had 2 cows and a mare and colt 1667.	CW 1663. Plague 3. <C>	Tenement with 1 acre, E of Roehampton-Barnes way, formerly occupied by Robert White 1676. Probably the R.A.W. who issued a trade token in 1659 saying 'The 3 Staggs Heads in Rohampton'. Inventory 1667: £31 + farming £11.[123] Rent £5 pa 1667.[124] (JD)
208	Thomas Birch	ex	7	Had a mare & colt, a sow and 2 pigs in 1668. (Note 22)	Head 1640, Con 1646, SH 1648, OP 1650-1, 1660, SH 1661, Con 1666, CW 1667. <C>	Inventory 1668: kitchen*, little room over cellar, red room*, parlour on N side, little buttery, little room under stairs, blue chamber on N side*, chamber over kitchen, chamber over steps, chamber over little room; £30.[125]
209	Nicholas [Richard] Waxham [Note 23]	ex	4	Brickmaker.	Side 1627, OP 1633, CW 1636-7, OP 1646-7/52, SH 1653, CW 1658-9. Small landholder. Aged 72. <C>	Tenement, W on the park pale of the Countess of Devonshire, E on the street, 1667; i.e. W of Roehampton Lane, mid-way between the present Cedars Cottages and Downshire House. But occupied cottage apparently E of Roehampton Street, 1663, and shared responsibility for scouring ditch from heath gate to Robert White's pales, 1656. (RW or JD)
210	Anthony Wilkins	ex	2		Former soldier. Ale 1665, Head 1668, Con 1670. Illit. <P?>	
211	[Widow] ... Norwood	ex	2		<C>	Tenement formerly occupied by Walter Norwood, 1675. He issued a trade token showing a rose crowned. Site is W of Roehampton Lane, just N of Downshire House. (JW)
212	Mrs [Susan] Poole wider	nulla bona	*4*		<C>	Tenement, 1688. Site is W of Roehampton Lane, where the N part of Downshire House now stands. Inventory 1674: £10.[126] (JD)
213	Mr Thomas Newthell [Nuthall]	ex	8	Gentleman; (estate steward).[127]	Vestryman. Con 1648, CW 1650-3, SH 1654, OP 1657, SH 1660. Aged 61. <R>	Mansion divided into 3, inc. part occupied by Freeman, 1664; in 1694, with No. 212, abutting W on Countess of Northumberland, E on street, N on Martha Munday [formerly Walter Norwood's], S on John Pettiward.[128] In 1674, 7 hearths in 2 houses. Site is now the S part of Downshire House. (JD)

214	Mr Cressett	empty	4	(Lawyer.)[129]	<C>	Cressett purchased the White Hart Inn and 101 acres in 1663.[130] This and Nos. 217-18 are clearly out of order.
215	Henry Goodwman [Goodman]	empty	3		Head 1664. <C>	
216	Mr John Freeman	ex	2	Tailor.	Ale 1658, Head 1661, Con 1668/77, OP 1683-4/94. Lit. Aged 32. <C>	As No. 213 (but also recorded separately, 1674). (JD)
217	Mr John Hulke	ex	6	Innholder & a groom of the King's hunting horses c.1680.[131] (Note 24)	Illit. <C>	Inn called White Hart or Halfway House in Roehampton Vale.[132] Inventory 1687: kitchen*, hall, parlour*, dining room*, little chamber over gatehouse, hanged chamber*, little chamber, chamber over hall*, garretts, tailor's room, milkhouse, butteries, wash-houses, 2 barns, granaries; £72 + farming stock £166.[133]
218	— [Robert] Martin	empty	2		<C>	'At halfe way house' (register 1665). Possibly the brick farmhouse of 1664, with hall, parlour, kitchen, wash-house, dairy, buttery, 5 lodging chambers over, stables and barn.[134]
219	Thomas Marsey	ex	2		<P>	
220	Mr [John] Dawes lord	one empty	2			(JD)
221	Thomas Butler	ex	2	Coachman to Countess of Devonshire.[135]	Illit. <C>	
222	John Plowman	ex	2	Farrier.[136]	Ale 1662, Con 1664, Side 1666-8, SH 1671, Con 1678. <C>	(JD)
223	— [Mary] Runnells widd	ex	2	Held 16 acres from Pettiward 1658.	<C>	Tenement with barn abutting N on Roehampton Street, S and W on Thaire, 1658 (abuttals incorrect, as later plans prove). Shared responsibility for scouring ditch from heath gate to Robert White's pales, 1656. Site is E of present Roehampton Lane between the limb factory and Beech Close.[137] Rent £26 pa 1669. (JP)
224	John Munday	ex	2		Head 1663, OP 1665-7, Con 1669/75. <C>	
225	Elizabeth Gilbert	ex	3		<C>	Gilbert, whose husband had leased Little Fangate, later married James Muggett (see No. 228). Rent £14 pa 1670. (JP)

226	John Squibb	nul bona	1	(Husband-man.) Had 6 cows, 1 calf, 1 hog, 1666.	Ale 1663, OP 1664. <C>	Inventory 1666: first room* [kitchen], second room [chamber]; £3 + farming £10.[138]
227	John Heath	ex	2	'Yeoman'.	Side 1661/4-5, Head 1667/9. Quaker 1672.[139] <C>	
228	Anne Medquicke [Magick; Muggett] wid	ex	4	Widow of gardener.	Quaker 1668. <C>	Possibly the tenement in New Field, recently erected in 1658, with 2 closes, abutting E on Stubfield Lane (now Holybourne Avenue), S on New Park wall, W on Blunt, formerly occupied by James Muggatt and others, 1716.[140] (JP)
229	John Clarke	ex	4		Head 1662, OP 1663, SH 1665-6. <C>	
230	Nicholas Gladwyn	ex	2	Husbandman. Had 5 cows, 2 calves, 2 hogs, 1 horse, poultry in 1687.	Con 1663, SH 1664, CW 1665, SH 1667, OP 1669-70, Con 1676, OP 1682. Pew. Lit. <C>	Tenement with 4 closes (15 acres) abutting S on New Park wall, N on common, E on premises formerly Benson's, W on Stubfield Lane, 1675.[141] Inventory 1687: kitchen*, room by kitchen, hall*, room over hall, room over kitchen, 'rooms over the rooms within [over?] the kitchin'; £11 + farming £19.[142] (JD)
231	Thomas Cudbeard	nulla bona	2		Ale 1661, Head 1671, Con 1674. <C>	
232	— Pennerd wid	nulla bona	2	Widow of yeoman.	<C>	
233	Arthur Munday	poore *+	1	Husbandman 1666;[143] victualler 1673; labourer 1678.	Aged 34. <P>	(4 hearths in 1664.)
234	Thomas Foster	poore*	1		Ale 1652, Con 1662. <P>	
235	George Peate [Pate]	empty	1	Carpenter.I	Head 1665. <P>	In 1617 Thomas Pate held 3 houses in Roehampton Street (on the site of the present entrance to Hartfield); perhaps the Pate family had retained them.[144]
236	Robert Higgoday	poore*	1	Labourer.	Ale 1656, Head 1666. <P>	In 1674 a cottage on manorial waste abutted N on Roehampton Street and E on the house of Robert Haggaday.[145]
237	George Gooderidge [Gutteridge]	poore*	1	Gardener 1683.	Ale 1676-8, Con 1683. <P>	
238	Anthony Lucas	poore*	2		Head 1649, Con 1651, Side 1652-3, OP 1654, SH 1655, Side 1658-9. <C>	

239	Mr Robins lord	empty	4			
240	Robert Dennis	burnt downe	2	Labourer. I	Ale 1664. <P>	
241	Phillip May	poore*	1		Ale 1654, Head 1656. <P>	
242	James Marnell	poore	1	I	Ale 1674-5. Casual poor relief 1660/1. Lit. <P*>	Shared responsibility for scouring ditch from heath gate to Robert White's pale, 1656 (if James Marscall was the 'Marnell' of 1665).
243	— [Anne] Gifford widow	nul bona [poor 1664]	4		Casual poor relief 1658/9. Illit. <P*>	Cottage with ½ acre, east of Roehampton-Barnes way, 1676. Shared responsibility for scouring ditch from heath gate to Robert White's pale, 1656.[146] (JD)
244	— Phillips widow	poore	1		<P*>	Perhaps the cottage abutting S on Samuel Snapes, N on Roehampton Street, W on house of John Dawes, E on house of Robert Haggaday, 1674. (MR)
245	John Cuffe	poore	1	Labourer.[147]	Head 1674. <P*>	Site of the present King's Head.[148]
246	— [Mary] White widow	poore+	2	I	Plague 3. <P>	
247	Giles Younge	poore*	2	Carpenter.	Ale 1657. Aged 29. <P>	
248	James Marsh	poore		Husbandman.[149]	Aged 78. <P*>	
249	— [Joan] Clarke widow	poore	1		Casual poor relief 1658-61. <P*>	Rent £1½ pa 1663/4.[150]
250	— Read widow	empty	1		Casual poor relief 1657/8. <P*>	Parish contributed £1 towards building the house 1651/2. Rent apparently 25s. in 1660.[151]
251	John Lawrence	poore	1	Labourer 1676.[152]	Ale 1669, Head 1672. <P*>	Cottage abutting S on the common, N on Thomas Nuthall, 1676. (MW)
252	— Perkins wid	poore	1		<P*>	'Living on the common side' (register 1659).
253	Henry Clifford	poore	1	Coachman 1654; husbandman 1656; labourer 1680.[153] I	Ale 1671, Head 1675. <P*>	Tenement and 1 rood (¼ acre or 40 rods) 1697; judging by its size, can only be the 30 rods of former waste later granted to Rebecca Baker and shown on later plans. Site is on N side of present Roehampton High Street.[154]
254	— [Grissell] Jennyngs wid	poore+	1	Had 3 cows, 1 calf, 1 bullock, 1673.	Quaker 1668. Casual poor relief 1668. <P*>	Inventory 1673: kitchen*, room by kitchen, chamber over kitchen, chamber by it; £5.[155]

255	John Deacon	poore	1		Casual poor relief 1660/1. <P*>	Probably cottage with 12 rods which Elizabeth Deacon, daughter of John, was licensed to hold in 1673, abutting N on John Dawes, S on the common, E on Hugh Roberts and W on Henry Harding. (Widow Roberts' cottage in 1707 was on the N side of Roehampton High Street near the E end, and itself abutted E on widow Harding's cottage.)[156] (MW)
256	Daniell Harding	poore	1	Husbandman.[157] I	Casual poor relief 1660/1. <P*>	Licensed 1666 to hold cottage and 10 rods of common land. (MW)
257	Capt. [John] Blunt lord[158]	emptie	10	(Had moved to No. 24.)	SH 1656.	Tenement with barns etc. and 2 closes totalling 10 acres. Site is W of Holybourne Avenue. (JB)
258	Humphrey Beare [Bare]	poore	1		<P*>	
P10	*Richard Smith*	*poor*	*1*			
P11	*John Monke*	*poor*	*1*			Accused of building a new cottage 1626; probably on the N side of the present High Street.[159]
P12	*Ralph Darell*	*poor*	*1*			
P13	*Frances Breed widd*	*poor*	*1*			

Index to the directory

Surnames have been standardised and sometimes corrected (as in the table). '(R)' indicates Roehampton.

Sources for the directory (see page 100 for abbreviations)

Name: TNA, E 179/188/489A. Forenames have been expanded where abbreviated. Corrections in square brackets are from the parish register or the 1662, 1664 or 1668 lists. Italics in this and the next two columns indicate information from the 1664 list or elsewhere.
Hearths and tax status: TNA, E 179/188/489A.
Occupation: The parish register, Surrey Quarter Sessions, the list of payments from Putney parish to watermen 1662-76 (in WLHS) and the list of watermen at sea 1672 (TNA, E 179/346), unless a reference is given; all from 1654-72 unless a date is given. Evidence on nurse children is from the parish register.
Status etc.: Vestry membership, parochial offices, pews and poor relief (except in 1673-4) are from CWA. Manorial offices are from WCR. Literacy and illiteracy are from wills (in NA and LPL) and Chancery depositions. Poor relief in 1673-4 is from WLHS, Putney overseers' accounts 1673/4. Plague deaths are from the parish register. Ages, where known, are from legal depositions (mostly in Chancery) and the parish register (the latter mainly for ages at death, since only eight baptisms of those listed in 1665 have been identified, partly because the register begins only in 1620).
Location: WCR, unless a reference is given. The initials in brackets at the end of each entry refer to the holder of the premises from the manor, and references in the manor court rolls to that person's holding are listed in Appendix 1. Some information is from the parish register, in which case 'register' is indicated in brackets. Rents are from William Wymondsold's notebook (NRO, Spencer papers, 7j5, Surveys 12) and John Pettiward's rent book for 1669-71 (in the possession of Michael Bull), unless a reference is given. Information on trade tokens is from G.C. Williamson, *Trade tokens in the seventeenth century* (1891), vol. 2, pp. 1144, 1147.

Notes to the directory

1. Held 7 acres of Gainsford land 1664, 2½ acres of Pettiward land 1666, 4 acres of Wymondsold land 1685, 6 acres of Pettiward land 1688.
2. Held Withy Croft 1657 (TNA, C 24/819, Platt v. Carter; TNA, C 24/828, Wymondsold v. Platt), 9 acres of Powell land (later Pettiward)1664, 8 acres of Wymondsold land 1685.
3. Held 16 acres of Wymondsold land by leases of 1650 and 1660 (£26 pa), Gainsford land 1664, 10 acres of Williams land 1682.
4. In the 1668 rate Hugh Harwood is between Davis and Ashfield instead of Costrell, and widow Howard was (with John Start) later an occupant of the Wymondsold tenement (then divided into two) which abutted N and E on the Point, S on the highway to Barnes and W on premises of Robert Wymondsold, and which in 1716 was leased to Andrew Combes, landlord of the Duke of Ormonde's Head (TNA, C 54/5383, No. 2; TNA, C 54/5316, No. 9).
5. Held 2½ acres of Wymondsold land in 1660s.
6. Leased close from William Wymondsold 1663 (£12 pa).
7. Inventory of William Salmon 1680: nursery, chamber over still house, chamber over hall, maids' chamber, chamber over wash house, chamber over kitchen, widow's closet, staircases, still house, men's chamber, coachman's chamber, laundry, withdrawing room, parlour, closet adjoining parlour, hall, buttery, kitchen, cellar (Corporation of London RO, Court of Orphans inventories, box 20). William Salmon was a son of Olive Yardley (TNA, PROB 11/216, Sir William Becher) and occupied the house in 1674.
8. Leased Withicroft Close from William Wymondsold 1650 (£8 pa).
9. In 1679 had 4 working horses, another horse, 3 mares, 2 colts, 11 cows, 10 hogs, 10 acres of turnips, 1 acre of parsnips and corn and hay.
10. Inventory of William Langhorne 1655: long gallery, little chamber next it, Mr Conyers' chamber*, 'the mens chamber', chamber next to it, little room, maids chamber next the great chamber, great chamber*, chamber over the dais*, drying room, closet next to it, three maids chambers, widow's chamber*, dining chamber*, chamber over great parlour*, chamber over [?], stair's head, counting house, great parlour*, hall*, little parlour*, buttery*, kitchen*, storehouse, dairy, stable, stable chamber, Mrs Langhorne's closet (TNA, PROB 2/433a).
11. Inventory of Sir John Lawrence 1692: drying room*, next garrett*, garrett next to that; garrett by stair's head, room with red wrought bed*, room with blue bed*, room next blue room, room with grey striped hangings*, cheese chamber, maids chamber*, nursery*, maids chamber*, dressing room and closet*, 'Ladyes chamber'*, great dining room*, room with white wrought bed at stair's head*, room at head of great stairs*, ditto*, great staircase, little parlour*, little room under great staircase, hall*, little room at end of hall, great parlour*, pantry, cellar, servants' hall*, brewhouse, still-house*, kitchen*, scullery, pantry, bakehouse, dairy house, cheese house, meal house, lumber house, long closet, laundry, closet within blue room, room over stables, gardener's lodge; £546 (TNA, PROB 5/2301).

12. Inventory of Dawes Wymondsold 1675: parlour*, black parlour*, withdrawing room, great parlour*, hall*, waiters' hall*, little room adjoining, still house, pantry, kitchen*, best chamber*, dressing room*, room over kitchen*, chamber over black parlour*, maid's chamber, dining room*, damask chamber*, dressing room, chamber over still house, chamber over part of hall, drawing room, white chamber*, chamber within white chamber, blue chamber*, chamber within blue chamber, upper gallery, linen room, study, balcony chamber*, wardrobe chamber*, garrett, maid's chamber, garrett*, stairs, pastry, cellars, dairy, wash house, room over dairy*; £627 (TNA, PROB 4/3128).
13. Inventory of Peter Proby 1684: garretts, gilt leather room*, sad coloured room*, long dining room*, green drugget room*, widow's chamber*, wardrobe*, closet adjoining, drying room, parlour next the street*, hall, parlour next the garden*, new parlour*, kitchen*, butteries, larder, cellar, wash house*, room over same, stable, coach houses, deceased's closet; £317 (TNA, PROB 5/1892).
14. Inventory of Roger Pettiward 1675: hall, little parlour, best parlour*, kitchen* & entry, wash-house, shoe-house, storehouse, dining room*, chamber over best parlour*, passage, chamber over kitchen*, little parlour chamber, closet over stone entry, little study, red chamber, nursery, great study, green chamber, 7 garretts, wash house; £410 (TNA, PROB 5/1894). In this inventory hearths are generally indicated only by bellows and there is a separate entry for 'three paire of brasse andirons, four paire with brasses four paire of doggs four fire shovells with tonges', so the inventory understates the number of hearths. Two hearths stated in 1665, evidently incorrectly.
15. Leased a garden (£5 pa) 1656 and 8 acres (£13.6s.8d. pa) 1662 from William Wymondsold; also 3 acres from Pettiward 1688.
16. Leased part of Coalecroft 1650 and 3 closes from William Wymondsold 1653 (£12 pa).
17. Held 12 acres of Wymondsold land 1685, 2 acres of former Teringham land 1685, part of Wymondsold's Manygate Close 1685.
18. Pension as maimed soldier wounded in service of Charles II by 1690 (SHC, QS 2/1/6, p. 384).
19. Leased Walnut Tree Close 1665 (WCR, Roll 150, 8 Apr 1665).
20. Occupied Goose Mead, 3 acres, 1673 (WCR, 369/1, 14 Apr 1673, Powell to Kentish).
21. Had 8 cows, 1 mare & colt, 1 sow, hay in barn and milk vessels, 1666. It is not always possible to distinguish Nicholas Waxham senior and junior. Nicholas Waxham junior was said to have left the parish in 1664.
22. Held 8 acres of Dawes land before 1676.
23. Richard Waxham was still a householder in Roehampton in 1667; in the 1664 list Richard (placed between Birch and Wilkins) has 4 hearths and Nicholas has 3.
24. Had 11 cows, 1 bull, 13 pigs, 5 horses, poultry and various crops in 1687.

Appendices

Appendix 1: Landholders in 1665

AR: Anne Rogers of Putney (part purchased from John Dawes 1663 or 1665): Roll 150, 11 June 1663, 14 Feb 1664/5; 369/5, 11 Apr 1687 (refers back to 1668).

DC: Dorothy Conyers widow and Oliver Conyers, citizen & skinner of London (inherited by Dunstan Duck's nephew William and his wife Dorothy 1652; Oliver was their son): Roll 147, 4 Apr 1654; Roll 150, 10 Apr 1664; 369/1, 26 Apr 1669; 369/4, 4 May 1685.

DW: Dawes Wymondsold (inherited from his grandfather, William Wymondsold 1664): Roll 149, 16 May 1662, 28 Apr 1663 (refers to William Wymondsold); Roll 150, 19 Apr 1667; 369/1, May 1670, 22 Apr 1672, 17 Feb 1674; 369/5, 14 July 1685; William Wymondsold's notebook, NRO, Spencer papers, 7j5, Surveys 12.

GP: George and Elizabeth Platt (inherited as son-in-law and daughter of Mathias Smyth, c.1657): Roll 150, 23 July 1664.

HG: Lady Hester Gainsford (inherited from mother Anne Hill, who inherited from John Hill of London, goldsmith, 1646, who obtained it by mortgage 1642): Roll 150, 22 Apr 1664; 369/1, 4 May 1674; 369/3, 15 Apr 1678.

HH: Hugh Hubbert of Putney, lord of the manor of Allfarthing, Wandsworth (part purchased from John Dawes 1641; remainder probably acquired as a creditor of Dawes): 369/1, 17 July 1669.

HN: Hugh Nicholls of Whitechapel (inherited from Christopher Nicholls 1656 or 1660): Roll 149, m. 2 (1656); 369/6, 18 May 1692.

JB: John Blunt of Stepney 1654, of Roehampton 1656, of Bristol 1668 (purchased 1654): Roll 147, 18 July 1654; Roll 149, m. 3a (1656).

JD: John Dawes (inherited from Sir Abraham Dawes): Roll 149, 2 Apr 1657 (refers to Robert Cole), m. 8b (1658), 28 Apr 1663; 369/1, 19 Feb 1674/5; 369/2, 22 Dec 1675, 4 May 1676; 369/5, 30 Apr 1688.

JL: Sir John Lawrence of London (purchased 1656): 369/5, 24 Sept 1685.

JP: John Pettiward (inherited from father-in-law Henry White 1658): Roll 147, 27 Aug 1646 (refers to White); Roll 149, 19 Oct 1658; Roll 150, 30 Apr 1666; 369/1, 26 Apr 1669, 16 Feb 1671/2.

JW: John Waterer, gentleman: 369/2, 22 Dec 1675.

JY: John Younge of London, gentleman (apparently mortgagee): Roll 150, 30 Apr 1666; 369/1, 27 June 1673 (refers to Lady Clarke).

MC: Mary Clarke, widow (widow of the holder in 1636): Roll 150, 30 Apr 1666 (property excepted from grant to Henry Young); 369/1, 27 June 1673; 369/6, 8 Apr 1695 (refers to Elizabeth Herbert); 369/7, 28 Apr 1707 (refers to George Garrett).

MN: Mary Norman (widow of William Norman, who purchased it from John Dawes 1650): Roll 147, 11 & 20 Apr 1650; 369/1, 14 Apr 1673.

MS: Mathias Smyth of Putney, chandler (inherited by his brother Stephen from Robert Boughton 1663): Roll 149, m. 18b (1663) (refers to Stephen Smyth); 369/1, 8 May 1671, 4 May 1674.

MW: Manorial waste: Roll 145, 5 May 1626; Roll 150, 30 Apr 1666, 11 Dec 1666; 369/1, 14 Apr 1673, 4 May 1674; 369/2, 3 July 1675, 23 May 1676.

RH: Robert Huntley (inherited by Mary Huntley from her father 1604): Roll 145, 5 May 1626; Roll 149, 7 Apr 1662; 369/1, 4 May 1674; 369/5, 30 Apr 1688.

RW: Richard Waxham of Roehampton (inherited; in Waxham hands by 1617): Roll 150, 19 Apr 1667.

SS: Stephen Smyth of London, mealman, or of Putney, tallow chandler (inherited from Mathias Smyth): Roll 147, 4 Apr 1654, Dec 1654; Roll 150, 8 Apr 1665, 4 May 1665; 369/1, 18 Apr 1670; 369/7, 3 Apr 1706 (Thomas Kentish's holding).

ST: Sarah Terringham, widow of James Martyn, then wife of Sir William Terringham (purchased by James Martyn from Thomas Hill 1650): Roll 147, 30 Aug 1652; 369/2, 22 Dec 1675.

TC: Sir Thomas Chamberlayne (purchased from Thomas Gough 1651): 369/1, 16 Feb 1671/2.

TJ: Thomas Juer of Putney, baker (purchased from Philip Bourne 1647): Roll 147, 3 May 1647; 369/3, 5 May 1679.

TK: Thomas Kentish, carpenter (purchased from Stephen Smyth 1665): see SS.

TM: Thomas Maund, citizen & lorimer of London (purchased from Philip Bourne 1647 and 1650): Roll 147, 3 May 1647, 20 Apr 1650; 369/1, 14 Apr 1673.

WG: William Garrett of Putney, waterman: Roll 146, 21 Apr 1642; Roll 150, 30 Apr 1666; 369/7, 15 Apr 1700 (refers to Thomas Garrett).

WH: William Harvey (inherited from Eliab Harvey 1662): Roll 147, m. 25b (1654); Roll 150, 7 Apr 1662.

WP: Sir William Powell (inherited; in Powell hands by 1636): Roll 147, 3 Sept 1649; 369/4, 14 Apr 1684; 369/5, 5 Oct 1685, 19 Apr 1686 (all these refer to John and Mary Williams).

WS: Walter Sisam of Putney, gardener (purchased from William Norman 1661): Roll 149, 15 Oct 1661.

WW: William Webb, citizen & merchant tailor of London (acquired Jan 1665): Roll 150, 23 July 1664 (refers to Pullein), 11 Jan 1665; 369/7, 9 May 1698.

Appendix 2: Plague deaths in 1665-7

First death	Later deaths	No. of deaths	Name of householder	Occupation of householder	Deaths	Hearths	Location
1665							
23 July	8 Aug	2	John Combes	Waterman	Wife, daughter		
26 July	6, 8(2), 10(2) Aug	6	Thomas Howell [senior]	Waterman	Man from; female parish child; wife; daughter; daughter; female nurse child	2 p	169
6 Aug	12 June 1666	2	Joseph Smith	Gardener	Male nurse child; nurse child [also son d. 30 May 1666; recently-born child d. July 1666]	1 p	66
14 Aug	27 Aug	2	[George] Dollard	Waterman	Woman at; mother of ditto		23A
27 Aug	10(2), 14 Sept	4	Hester Symonds	Butcher	Self; Matthew Symonds; James Symonds; daughter	2	30
29 Aug	2 Sept	2	Mary Silley widow	Widow of waterman	Daughter; self	1 p	75
29 Aug	23 Jan	2	Mr Axtel		Child at; child at		
1 Sept	14 Sept	2	Thomas Harwood	Waterman	Daughter; nurse boy	2 p	178
4 Sept	4 Sept	2	Susanna Cooke widow	Widow of waterman	Self; daughter	4	29
4 Sept		1	Richard Ironmonger		Self	2	79
5 Sept	19 Sept	2	Robert Combes	Waterman	Manservant; wife [house shut up 1 Sept]	4	20A
6 Sept	16 Sept	2	Thomas Seers	Waterman	Manservant; son	1	50A
6 Sept	13 Sept	2	Widow Williams		Son; daughter	p	
14 Sept	28 Sept, 1, 2(2), 10 Oct	6	William Young	Basketmaker	Self; daughter; chrisom child; widow; son; daughter	2 p	44
18 Sept (2)	19 Sept, 3 Oct	4	Mary Marquis	Widow of victualler	Self; son; brother; son	6 inn	36
21 Sept	10, 26 Dec	3	Robert White	Innholder	Son; servantmaid; daughter	6 inn	207 (R)
23 Sept	27 Sept, 7 Oct	3	Widow White		Son; self; nurse child	2	246 (R)
1 Oct		1	Henry Tunstall	Glasier	Son	5	184
1 Oct		1	Thomas Silley	Husbandman	Nurse child	1	129A

1 Oct	21 Oct, 3, 4 Nov	4	[Richard] Higginbottom	Tailor	Apprentice; son; son; wife	2	19
1 Oct		1	Thomas Kite	Innholder	Daughter	12 inn	32
6 Oct		1	William Garrett	Waterman	Self	2	156
8 Oct		1	[Richard] Keffe	Waterman/ labourer	William Kemp's child nursed at Keffe's	1 p	105
9 Oct	26, 29 Oct	3	William Butterfield	Waterman	Daughter; wife; daughter	1	37A
11 Oct	11 Oct	2	William Fisher	Waterman	Son; female servant	1	69
12 Oct		1	Richard Tunstall	Waterman	Son [self d. 21 Jan 1666]	2	39
14 Oct		1	Henry Driver	Victualler	Daughter	4 ale	181
16 Oct		1	Widow Forth		Daughter	1 p	97
27 Oct		1	Hugh Harwood	Waterman	Daughter		23B
18 Nov		1	Anne Rogers widow		Daughter		
19 Nov	28 Nov	2	Richard Blackburne		Son; wife		
29 Nov	11, 26 Oct 1666, 18 Feb 1667	4	Richard Crane	Bricklayer	Daughter; son; son; manservant	2	91
12 Dec		1	Nicholas Waxham	Husbandman	Son	3	206 (R)
1666							
4 Jan (2)	10 Jan	3	Robert Cooke		Self; son; daughter [also daughter d. 10 Dec]	3	41
8 Jan		1	Renolls Bowles		Self		
22 Feb		1	Hugh Williams	Labourer	Son	1 p	P1
26 Mar	10 Apr	2	Thomas Char	Waterman	Daughter; woman from	1	46
10 Apr	18 Apr	2	Simon Mowden	Waterman	Wife; daughter	1 p	45
11 Apr	23, 28, 29 Apr	4	Philip Howard	Waterman	Daughter; son; wife; daughter	2	49
19 May		1	John Costrells	Victualler	Boy from	2 ale	9

Notes: The source is the parish register. 'p' indicates householders among the poorest 53 in Putney (or, in the case of widow Williams, receipt of casual poor relief in 1665-6). 'ale' and 'inn' indicate alehouses and inns. Additional deaths noted here in square brackets are ones for which the parish register does not indicate plague as the cause.

Appendix 3: Hearth tax lists for Putney parish

The 1662 list is a house-by-house one, but many householders are listed separately (also in house-by-house order) as not having paid and are included here; the exempt are not listed. The 1664 list groups all the merchants and gentlemen together at the beginning, and also lists those exempt separately; however, both the lesser houses and (separately) the exempt appear to be listed in house-by-house order. The figures for 1665 in the table include only dwellings actually listed, and not those added in the directory above; those recorded in the table as 'exempt' are those counted above as the poorest householders. The 1674 list appears to have been compiled from a house-by-house list, but seems unreliable in that respect; it does not list the exempt. An undated Putney list has 118 names, all chargeable, but is clearly incomplete (TNA, E 179/384/19). A list for 1673 is almost identical to the 1674 one (TNA, E 179/188/504). A Roehampton list of c.1665/6 lists 25 chargeable and 21 'paupers & not chargeable', but may be incomplete (TNA, E 179/258/4). No Roehampton list survives for 1662.

Hearths	20 +	10-19	7-9	6	5	4	3	2	1	ex 3+.	ex 2	ex 1	?	Total non-exempt	Total inc. exempt
Putney															
1662	3	17	18	7	6	12	12	65	3					143	
1664	3	17	11	5	8	13	17	63	13	2	26	19		150	197
1665	3	18	12	10	4	13	17	73	8	3	21	13	2	160	197
1674	3	20	9	7	8	25	22	76	8					178	210¶
Roehampton															
1664	2	1	2	2	0	7	6	16	9	1*	2	13		45	61
1665	2	1	3	2	0	6	3	19	9	1	2	12		45	60
1674	2	1	2	1	1	10	7	6	1					31	49¶

* Includes one 4-hearth house.
¶ Exempt added from certificate of *1672* (TNA, E 179/346).
Sources: TNA, E 179/257/29; TNA, E 179/188/481; TNA, E 179/188/489A; TNA, E 179/188/496.

Notes

Abbreviations: **1617 survey** - NRO, survey of Wimbledon manor, 1617; **1664 list** - TNA, E 179/188/481; **1668 rate** - CWA, ff. 394-6; **CWA** - Putney churchwardens' accounts, 1623-93, LMA, P95/MRY1/413; **LMA** - London Metropolitan Archives; **LPL** - Lambeth Palace Library; **NRO** - Northamptonshire Record Office; **QS** - Surrey County Council, *Surrey Quarter Sessions records*, vols. 6-9 (1934/5/8/51) for 1659-68; typescript at SHC for 1669-91; **Register** - A.C. Hare (ed.), *The parish register of Putney*, Surrey Parish Register Society, vols. 11-13 (1913-16); **RO** - Record Office or Records Office; **SHC** - Surrey History Centre; **TNA** – The National Archives; **WLHS** - Wandsworth Local History Service; **Williamson** - G.C. Williamson, *Trade tokens in the seventeenth century* (1891), vol.2; **Woodhead** - J.R. Woodhead, *The rulers of London 1660-1689* (1965). No footnotes are given in the text if they are provided in the directory instead.

PART I

Chapter 1: The hearth tax and its records (pages 7-13)

1. QS, 1663-6, p. 122. **2.** Rogers' name appears at the end of the 1665 list as constable, together with Robert Pope, headborough, though these were not elected as such in 1664 or 1665, and Pope is not in the list itself as a householder. There is a similar problem in the Roehampton list with Nicholas Gladwyn, constable, and John Green, headborough. The Putney and Roehampton lists were made for the Ladyday 1665 collection (25 March), the Roehampton list being headed as such, but appear to have been compiled slightly later, i.e. after the death of Edward Gilbert on or about 2 April (since Gilbert's widow is listed) and before the death of Mary Holton, widow (buried on 20 July). **3.** Not until 1684 were collectors ordered to make house-by-house lists (Duncan Harrington (ed.), *Kent hearth tax assessment Lady Day 1664* (British Record Society, Hearth Tax Series vol. 2, 2000), p. xxi). For a local example (the 1664 list for Richmond) analysed in detail, see John Cloake, *Cottages and common fields of Richmond and Kew* (2001), pp. 147-210. **4.** Most of the Wymondsold holding – the largest – is not recorded in detail between 1629 and 1685. **5.** Notably as regards the row of eight dwellings on the corner of Felsham Road (Nos. 55-59A; only five listed in 1665) and the seven dwellings on one of the Lower Richmond Road sites (Nos. 20A-23C; only three listed in 1665). **6.** Excluding widow Hendings, assumed to be the Helen Hitens of Roehampton, who died in April 1665, and widow Tyler, who had entered the almshouse in Putney. Omitting some of the poor was not unusual: see M.J. Power, 'The social topography of Restoration London', in A.L. Beier and Roger Finlay (eds.), *London 1500-1700: the making of the metropolis* (1986), pp. 200-1. **7.** Eleven recipients of poor relief in 1665/6 are not in the list, but only for two of them is there evidence at any date of them being a householder, so these are not added. They included Ellen Jones, for whom there is an inventory, indicating a two-room house, but not until 1669; John Austen, who occupied one of Mary Clarke's tenements (Nos. 25-7) in April 1666 (WCR, Roll 150, 30 Apr 1666), but is not in the 1664 or 1668 lists; and Widow Pascall, whose rent of £1.10s.0d. per year (to Nicholas Meade) in 1662-4 suggests she was a lodger (CWA, pp. 341, 345). **8.** i.e. Nos. 20A, 23A, 23B, 37A, 50A, 55A, 129A, 129B, 170A. Five of these are where the manor court roll in or about 1665 records more dwellings than there are householders listed in 1665, and six headed households where there were plague deaths in 1665-6. Sources are: Combes 1664 list, 1664/5 court roll, 1665 register, 1668 rate; Dollard and Harwood 1664/5 court roll, 1665 register; Butterfield 1664 list, 1665 register; Seers 1664 list, 1665 register, 1668 rate, 1669 court roll; Char 1664 list, court roll 1664/9; Silley 1664 list, 1665 register, 1668 rate; Robins QS 1663-6 p. 214, 1668 rate; Fisher 1664 list, 1665 court roll. **9.** e.g. several listed in 1664 or 1668 but not both, such as William Milborne, fisherman (1664 only; date of death unknown), widow Dias (1664 only; received poor relief in 1668) and Henry Ford, barber/labourer (1668 only). George Platt, waterman, owned the Queen's Head site (Nos. 40-3), but is not listed in the court roll for July 1664 among its occupants; he is listed near John Martin (No. 61) in 1664 and at the Queen's Head in 1668. Goodman Roberts of Roehampton, who had a death in his household in 1665, may have been in Cottage Row (WCR, 369/1, 6 Apr 1669). **10.** Robert Latham and William Matthews (ed.), *The diary of Samuel Pepys* (1970-83), vol. 1, 24 Aug 1660, vol. 2, 12 June 1661, vol. 3, 27 Oct 1662. **11.** Location identified from his place in the 1668 rate. **12.** TNA, PROB 24/10, ff. 324, 327, 604, 650; TNA, C 8/176/97; TNA, PROB 11/338, Thomas Bunn. **13.** http:/longislandgenealogy.com/conklin.

Chapter 2. Putney and Roehampton in 1665 (pages 14-21)

1. East Sussex RO, FRE 501. **2.** TNA, E 133/84/58. **3.** Dorian Gerhold, *Putney in 1636: Nicholas Lane's map* (1994), p. 23. **4.** TNA, C 24/661, Bradborne v. Wymondsold, p. 36. **5.** 1617 survey; WLHS, Putney poor rate books. 6. CWA, ff. 16, 21; CWA, pp. 385-6, 397. **7.** The breakdown of the traditional system is indicated by the engrossing of a large proportion of the 'lots' in Putney's common meadow known as West Mead (by the river in Barnes) by William Wymondsold in the 1640s (WCR, 369/8, 19 April 1708). See also TNA, C 5/29/175. **8.** Latham and Matthews, *Diary of Samuel Pepys*, vol. 8, 7 May 1667. **9.** Based on the Surrey hearth tax list for 1674 (TNA, E179/188/496). **10.** See Dorian Gerhold, *Roehampton in 1617: the village surveyed* (2001), pp. 11-

18. **11.** *Ibid.*, pp. 11, 34. **12.** *Ibid.*, pp. 25, 44 n89. **13.** British Library, Althorp Papers, P13, Part 1, Section 1, plan of Putney Park 1753; TNA, C 43/213, m. 6; Worcester Cathedral Library, D634. **14.** See TNA, PROB 24/10, f. 327. After the 1660s the number of baptisms fails to keep up with the rising population, judging by the Putney rate for 1736 (at WLHS). **15.** Tom Arkell, 'A method for estimating population totals from the Compton census returns', in Kevin Schurer and Tom Arkell (eds.), *Surveying the people* (1992), p. 98. **16.** Peter Laslett, *The world we have lost – further explored* (1983), p. 32; Tom Arkell, 'Illuminations and distortions: Gregory King's scheme calculated for the year 1688 and the social structure of later Stuart England', *Economic History Review*, vol. 59 (2006), pp. 62-3. See also Peter Earle, *The making of the English middle class* (1989), pp. 214-17; J.T. Cliffe, *The world of the country house in seventeenth-century England* (1999), pp. 198-202. **17.** Below; TNA, C 10/1/13. **18.** Craig Spence, *London in the 1690s: a social atlas* (2000), p. 64. **19.** Daniel Lysons, *The environs of London* (1792), vol. 1, p. 417. **20.** The figure based on the hearth tax ignores the fact that some houses were described as empty. **21.** In seven cases the landlord is listed in place of the occupant, and in two cases the occupant had moved and appears elsewhere in the list. **22.** *The Post-Man*, 16-18 March 1703; *Daily Courant*, 5 April 1704. **23.** See Gerhold, *Putney in 1636*, pp. 43-8. **24.** 67 net, since some plots had fewer houses than in 1617; 75 houses had been added and eight had gone. The unlocated houses in the directory below are included if their approximate location is known. **25.** WCR, Roll 150, 22 April and 23 July 1664, 8 April 1665, 19 April 1667; WCR, 369/7, 1 May 1704. **26.** TNA, C 7/191/105; TNA, C 3/449/74; WCR, 369/3, 18 April 1681. **27.** WCR, Roll 149, 19 Oct 1658; QS, 1661-3, p. 305; John Pettiward's rent book for 1669-71, in possession of Michael Bull. **28.** WCR, Roll 147, 16 April 1649, Powell to Powell. **29.** There was a gardener, John Cole, at about No. 86 in 1668. **30.** See Gerhold, *Roehampton surveyed*, pp. 31-4. **31.** TNA, E 179/188/496; WLHS, Roehampton rate, 1713. **32.** Tom Arkell, 'Identifying regional variations from the hearth tax', *Local Historian*, vol. 33 (2003), pp. 153-4. **33.** The 1664 figures are 39%, 34% and 38% respectively. **34.** Arkell, 'Identifying regional variations', pp. 156, 158, 166-7. **35.** Excluding suburban or nearly suburban parishes as far out as Kensington. The comparison is based on hearth tax lists mainly of c.1674, especially TNA, E 179/188/496; TNA, E 179/143/370; TNA, E 179/246/22; TNA, E 179/129/746; TNA, E 179/249/25/1. The number of such houses *per acre* exceeded Putney's figure in 11 parishes. **36.** Arkell, 'Identifying regional variations', pp. 156, 166. The 1664 figures for Putney parish are used here instead of 1665 because more reliable; see below. **37.** Based on figures in C.A.F. Meekings (ed.), *Surrey hearth tax 1664* (Surrey Record Society, vol. 17, 1940).

Chapter 3. The people (pages 22-35)

1. LPL, COMM V/5, p. 302; Latham and Matthews, *Diary of Samuel Pepys*, vol. 8, 25 Aug 1667. **2.** CWA, p. 358. Contributors who were not householders in Putney are ignored here. **3.** Gerhold, *Putney in 1636*, pp. 10-11, 37. **4.** Woodhead, p. 106; *Gentleman's Magazine* (1769), p. 515. **5.** Woodhead, p. 129; WCR, Roll 149, m. 9-10; Gerhold, *Putney in 1636*, pp. 37-8; SHC, land taxes for Putney. **6.** Woodhead, pp. 44, 47, 71. This is a correction of the statement in Gerhold, *Putney in 1636* , p. 18 about Burlamachi's residence; see Dorian Gerhold, *The great houses of Putney* (Wandsworth Paper, in preparation). **7.** British Library, Add 24064, f. 12; *Oxford dictionary of national biography*. **8.** TNA, PROB 11/375, John Hingeston; Latham and Matthews, *Diary of Samuel Pepys*, vol. 7, 19 Dec 1666 and note. **9.** *Oxford dictionary of national biography*; register; WCR, Roll 146, 1 Sept 1641; LMA, P95/MRY1/414, f. 59. **10.** Corporation of London RO, Orphans' inventories 692. **11.** This and subsequent percentages are based on 210 of the 222 dwellings, excluding Nos. 23, 47, 53, 101, 107-8, 116, 129, 158, 185, 196-7 (mainly those where the landowner appears to be listed rather than the occupant). **12.** Daniel Defoe, *A tour through the whole island of Great Britain* (1971 Penguin edn.), p. 177. **13.** TNA, PROB 5/1894. **14.** CWA, f. 89; CWA, p. 377. **15.** On the assumption of nine people per household, but more for knights and schools; see note 16 to Chapter 2. **16.** TNA, PROB 24/10, f. 650. **17.** TNA, PROB 5/1895. **18.** A few of the better-off apparently did not pay for pews (e.g. Nos. 22, 96, 120, 127, 149), and a few exempt in 1664 did pay (Nos. 70, 155, P7, P8). Some did not acquire pews because they died between 1665 and 1668. **19.** Register. **20.** i.e. 12 or more hearths, five at £105-£627; six-seven hearths, five at £30-£42 and one at £72; four hearths, six at £4-£19 and one at £34; three hearths, two at £6-£14; two hearths, 13 at £4-£21 and one at £66; one hearth, two at £3-£5. **21.** TNA, PROB 4/15195; LPL, VH 96/1426; LPL, VH 96/946. **22.** Arkell, 'Identifying regional variations', pp. 148-9. **23.** See below. **24.** Excluding four who were exempt in 1664 but not listed as poor in 1665 (Nos. 60, 70, 124, 155). Six of the exempt of 1664 were listed as chargeable in 1662, but all except one were among those who had not in fact paid; the exception was John Bryan (No. 57). **25.** Also excluding Nos. 38, 47, 83, 168, but including Nos. 65, 138. **26.** 157 householders were listed as chargeable in 1668, out of perhaps 217 in total (allowing for an increase of about seven since 1665). **27.** TNA, E 179/346. Those listed in 1665 who were pressed were Jeremiah Jones, Richard Penn, Thomas Char, William Char, William Holton, George Dollard, Edward Matthews and Simon Mowden, plus the servants of widow Francombe and widow Eldridge; Robert Lawson and Edward Crosted had gone to sea.

28. CWA, pp. 365, 368. Two who received poor relief paid tax or rates in 1664 or 1668 (Nos. 65, 138), but this is probably accounted for by changing circumstances. **29.** SHC, QS 2/1/5, pp. 159, 183, 265-6; WLHS, account of money paid by Putney overseers to watermen 1662-76. **30.** Tom Arkell, 'Understanding exemption from the hearth tax', in P.S. Barnwell and Malcolm Airs, *Houses and the hearth tax: the later Stuart house and society* (2006), p. 19. **31.** LPL, VH 97/1, p. 288. **32.** Nos. 113, 138, 169, 178A, 194, P2, P3, P5. **33.** The total poor rate was only £29 in 1659 and £35 in 1669 (LPL, VP 1C/2), and, since pensions were typically 12d. or 18d. per week, there could not have been more than about 12 pensioners even if all pensions were 12d. and pensions accounted for the entire poor rate. In 1681 there were 12 pensioners, costing the parish 13s. per week or about £34 for the year (CWA, pp. 483-4). Doubling the 12 in order to account (arbitrarily) for children, about 2% of the population received pensions, which appears to have been typical of rural parishes (Arkell, 'Illuminations', pp. 60-1). **34.** Arkell, 'Understanding exemption', p. 19; Steve Hindle, *On the parish? The micro-politics of poor relief in rural England c.1550-1750* (2004), pp. 271-2. **35.** CWA, p. 360. **36.** LPL, VH 96/2928. **37.** Lane's map; LMA, P95/MRY1/414, f. 1. **38.** British Library, Add 34718 to 34720. **39.** Noel Malcolm (ed.), *The correspondence of Thomas Hobbes*, vol. 2 (1994), p. 810. **40.** *Historic Manuscripts Commission*, vol. 5, p. 205a. **41.** Thomas Pomfret, *The life of the Right Honourable and religious lady Christian late Countess Dowager of Devonshire* (1685), pp. 33, 83. **42.** TNA, PROB 11/348, Dowager Countess of Devonshire. **43.** TNA, PROB 11/338, Thomas Butler. **44.** J. Tudor Lewis, 'Harvey: the scene of his last years and hours', *Medical History*, vol. 4 (1960), pp. 18-19, 21; WCR, Roll 149, 7 April 1662. **45.** John Monke (No. P11) is included in these figures. **46.** As in Putney, some of those described in the list as poor paid tax or rates in other years (ten householders), though one of these (No. 254) received poor relief in 1668 and so is counted here as among the poorest. Widow Gifford also received poor relief and was exempt in 1664, so is counted likewise. **47.** Pomfret, *Life*, p. 89. **48.** Nos. 220, 239, 257 are excluded from these figures. **49.** TNA, C 24/1412, Pettiward v. Bagnall, evidence of Susannah Hulke; TNA, PROB 4/12415. **50.** Kingston parish register, 1670, 1671. **51.** CWA, p. 400. **52.** i.e. 17%, compared with 21% in Roehampton. Obviously it is not always possible to distinguish fathers and sons with the same name. **53.** Excluded because they cannot be compared with those in 1674, when the exempt are not recorded. **54.** Peter Laslett, *Family life and illicit love in earlier generations* (1977), p. 99. Known relations such as widows have been counted as if the householder of 1665 was still in Putney in 1674.

Chapter 4. Earning a living (pages 36-43)

1. Dorian Gerhold, *Wandsworth past* (1998), p. 22; Cloake, *Cottages and common fields*, p. 225 (excluding the Londoners recorded there). **2.** TNA, PROB 4/2882. **3.** WCR, roll 150, 30 April 1666; Corris's map of Putney 1787 (in Wandsworth Museum) with NRO, Spencer 7h4 (book of reference). **4.** This includes the four described both as labourer and something else. **5.** CWA, p. 360. **6.** See Nos. 105, 188, P9. **7.** See Malcolm Thick, 'Market gardening in England and Wales', in Joan Thirsk (ed.), *The agrarian history of England and Wales*, vol. 5 (1984-5), chapter 18. **8.** WCR, 369/4, 14 April 1684, Williams to Harvey; WCR, 369/5, 14 July 1685, Wymondsold, 5 Oct 1685, Williams to Courtney, 30 April 1688, Pettiward to Dawes. **9.** LPL, VH 96/1488. **10.** *Extracts from the court rolls of the manor of Wimbledon*, part 1 (1866), pp. 101, 103, 105, 111, 127, 161, 185, 209. **11.** TNA, PROB 11/252, Sir Thomas Dawes. **12.** CWA, f. 397. **13.** Register, 1665. See Dorian Gerhold, 'Black people in 17th and 18th century Putney', *Wandsworth Historian*, No. 42 (1984), pp. 1-2. **14.** Charles James Ferèt, *Fulham old and new* (1900), vol. 1, p. 46. **15.** J.F. Willard and H.C Johnson (eds.), *Surrey taxation returns*, Surrey Record Society, vol. 11 (1932), p. 85. **16.** TNA, PROB 11/334, James White. **17.** Dorian Gerhold, 'The schools of 17th century Putney', *Putney Society Review*, No. 5 (1979), pp. 9-11; register, burials, 1672; TNA, C 10/1/13; LMA, P95/MRY1/414, f. 59; below. **18.** Latham and Matthews, *Diary of Samuel Pepys*, vol. 8, 28 April 1667. **19.** QS, 1663-6, p. 151, 1666-8, p. 138, 1678-82, p. 10; SHC, QS 2/1/6, p. 197. **20.** East Sussex Record Office, FRE 527. This was almost certainly Margaret Hayes, wife of John (No. 117). **21.** WCR, 369/1, 26 April 1669. **22.** Roger Finlay and Beatrice Shearer, 'Population growth and suburban expansion', in Beier and Finlay, *London 1500-1700*, p. 39. **23.** Peter Earle, *A city full of people: men and women of London 1650-1750* (1994), p.120. **24.** *Ibid.*, pp. 115-7. **25.** See Gillian Clark, 'A study of nurse children, 1550-1750', *Local Population Studies*, No. 39 (1987), pp. 8-23. **26.** QS, 1663-6, p. 201. **27.** CWA, pp. 388, 442. See also British Library, Add 18986, f. 180. **28.** CWA, p. 438.

Chapter 5. The houses (pages 45-54)

1. Gerhold, *Putney in 1636*, pp. 16-17; TNA, C 24/661, Bradborne v. Wymondsold, p. 36; Guildhall Library, MS 8674/58, p. 51, policy 44775. I am grateful to Tony Evans for the latter reference. **2.** WCR, 369/13, 12 July 1721; James Edwards, *Companion from London to Brighthelmston* (1801), p. 30. **3.** For similar house-plans for people not listed in 1665, see LPL, VH 96/1453, 1558, 1559, 1566, 1760, 2344. **4.** Three sons born between 1637 and 1645 are assumed to have left home. **5.** Register, burials, 6 Sept 1665. **6.** Peter Guillery, 'London's suburbs, house size and the hearth tax', in Barnwell, *Houses*, p. 45. **7.** By 1683 the bed in the kitchen had been moved to the chamber.

8. Harrington, *Kent hearth tax assessment*, p. lxv. **9.** See *ibid.*, p. lxxvii. **10.** LPL, VH 96/1488. **11.** 1617 survey; TNA, C 24/819, Platt v. Carter; TNA, C 24/820, Carter v. Platt; QS, 1666-8, p. 244. **12.** CWA, pp. 377, 387, 407. **13.** 1617 survey; TNA, C 2/Jas I/E6/76. **14.** CWA, ff. 2, 51; CWA, f. 419; SHC, 212/84/5 & 6. **15.** WLHS, Putney rate book, between 1807 and 1808 rates, valuation of new buildings 1815. **16.** Register. **17.** CWA, f. 50; WCR, Roll 145, 7 April 1628, 14 April 1629; WCR, 369/5, 14 July 1685, Wymondsold. **18.** Nos. 130, 159, 223, 225. **19.** Nos. 37, 84, 85, 113, 153, 181. **20.** Nos. 38, 70, 112, 120. **21.** CWA, pp. 387, 434, 436; WLHS, Putney overseers' accounts 1673/4. **22.** CWA, pp. 345, 436; WLHS, Putney overseers' accounts 1673/4. **23.** TNA, E 179/346. **24.** Earle, *City full of people*, p. 168. **25.** TNA, PROB 11/184, Abraham Dawes; British Library, Add 34718. **26.** Of the 26 reasonably detailed inventories from 1661 to 1680 inclusive, nine mention coal, six mention what appears to be firewood, and 16 mention neither.

Chapter 6. Inns and alehouses (pages 55-6)
1. 17-18 and 14-15 in 1721-7 and 1786-1830 respectively in Putney and three in both periods in Roehampton (except that none are listed for Roehampton in 1725) (SHC, QS 2/6 1721 Easter 80 & 81; SHC, QS 2/6 1725 Easter 37; SHC, QS 2/6 1727 Easter 55A; WLHS, West Brixton petty sessions minutes, 1786-1830). No. 137 is excluded from the figure for 1665. **2.** e.g. CWA, ff. 70, 80, 94. **3.** TNA, C 7/79/39. **4.** QS, 1669-70, p. 47. **5.** TNA, PROB 11/170, William Clifton; TNA, PROB 11/179, Bridget Clifton; SHC, 176/2/1 to 3. **6.** TNA, C 5/85/96. **7.** Williamson, p. 1144; QS, 1659-61, p. 132. **8.** Guildhall Library, MS 11936, vol. 16, p. 185. **9.** SHC, QS 2/6 1714/124. **10.** British Library, Eg 3392, f. 18.

Chapter 7. Office holding (page 57)
1. Names of manorial office-holders are missing or incomplete for 1631-9, 1642, 1655 and 1659-60, and those of parish ones for 1642, 1649 and 1662. **2.** W.E. Tate, *The parish chest* (1983 edn.), pp. 31-2. **3.** The average number of hearths of those holding each office (ignoring any hearths exceeding six) was: surveyor of the highways 3.8, constable 3.6, overseer of the poor 3.4, aleconner 2.9, sidesman 2.7, headborough 2.5. **4.** See chapter 1, note 2 above.

Chapter 8. The plague (pages 58-62)
1. Paul Slack, *The impact of plague in Tudor and Stuart England* (1985), pp. 150-1. **2.** Stephen Porter, *The great plague* (1999), p. 40. **3.** This section is based on the register and CWA, pp. 354-66. **4.** A John Combes, waterman, died in 1656, but it would not have been usual for the register to have referred in 1665 to his wife and daughter, as opposed to his widow and her daughter; possibly John Combes and his family were lodgers in 1665. **5.** CWA, p. 350. **6.** i.e. the number of deaths divided by the annual average of deaths over the previous decade. **7.** London figures from Porter, *Great Plague*, p. 76; Wandsworth and Putney figures from parish registers. Excess mortality in 1666 was 2.8 in Wandsworth and 1.5 in Putney parish. **8.** Some of those who died may have been lodgers in households already counted here. **9.** Porter, *Great Plague*, p. 62. **10.** Counting only households whose heads would have been included in the table of male employment in chapter 4 above. **11.** The figures cover only those households identifiable in the 1665 list. **12.** NRO, SOX 281, 1784 lease; *Parliamentary Papers*, 1901 vol. 51, p. 754.

PART II
Directory of householders in 1665 (pages 63-88)

1. Nos. 23A, 23B, 129B. **2.** Nos. 9, 24, 144, 201, 212. No. 147 is corrected from the 1664 list. **3.** The years given are the years when elected. **4.** Victualler in Mortlake 1654 (WCR, Roll 147, 4 Apr 1654). **5.** Corporation of London RO, Orphans inventories 130. That this is the correct Thomas Davis is indicated by debts owed to him by William Milborne, as well as by Thomas Bunn and Mrs Yardley. **6.** CWA, p. 285. **7.** *Oxford dictionary of national biography*; register 1650. **8.** See also East Sussex RO, FRE 526, Sept 1677. **9.** LPL, VH 96/623; LPL, VH 96/624. The later inventory is his widow's. Only the latter indicates a fire in the chamber. **10.** LPL, VH 96/598. **11.** See Appendix 1. **12.** Widow Haughton was occupant of one of Webb's seven tenements in Jan 1665. **13.** Purser was also listed with Crucher as occupant of one of Wymondsold's two tenements by the ferry place, but this was in 1685. **14.** TNA, PROB 4/2882. **15.** LPL, VH 97/1, p. 39. **16.** LPL, VH 96/2522; LPL, VH 96/2124. **17.** TNA, C 7/524/47. **18.** TNA, C 10/79/23. **19.** LPL, VH 96/2234. **20.** 1617 survey; TNA, C 54/5316, No. 3. **21.** TNA, PROB 4/4061. **22.** TNA, C 24/908, Freeston v. Blount, evidence of John Freeman. **23.** His widow paid rates in 1668. **24.** CWA, p. 361. **25.** TNA, C 24/819, Platt v. Carter. **26.** QS, 1661-3, p. 260. **27.** LPL, VH 96/2928. **28.** British Library, Add 18986, f. 180. **29.** See Dorian Gerhold, 'Allfarthing's missing manorial lords', *Wandsworth Historian*, No. 78 (2004), pp. 7-11. **30.** Corporation of London RO, Orphans' inventories, box 23. **31.** *Ibid.* **32.** TNA, PROB 11/375, John Hingeston. **33.** TNA, C 3/449/74; WCR, 369/1, 4 May 1674. **34.** LPL, VH 96/1427. The value of Thomas Juer's own inventory just two years earlier was only £2 (LPL, VH 96/1426). **35.** There were two James Embertons – senior and junior; one was aged

29 in 1665. **36.** TNA, E 179/384/19. There was uncertainty about whether blacksmiths' forges were chargeable. **37.** LPL, VH 96/876. **38.** Chargeable in 1662; exempt in 1664. **39.** Tailor in 1651. **40.** The other dwelling, between Fisher and Selby, was William Fisher's in 1664, but he was at No. 69 in 1665. **41.** Poor in 1664, but a ratepayer in 1668. **42.** Register; WCR, 369/1, 4 May 1674. **43.** QS, 1663-6, p. 176. **44.** NRO, Spencer books, 7j5, Surveys 12. **45.** CWA, p. 365. **46.** CWA, p. 363. The transfer from Carter to Platt has not been traced. **47.** LPL, VH 96/130. **48.** Woodhead, p. 57. 'Allder Ridger' in the 1664 list. **49.** WCR Roll 149, 19 Oct 1658, identifies this Francis Fisher as the bricklayer, rather than the brewer of the same name. **50.** LPL, VH 96/1125. **51.** QS, 1663-6, p. 201. **52.** WCR, 369/3, 5 May 1679; CWA, pp. 434, 436. **53.** The order of the names given in 1658 does not correspond to that in the 1665 tax list. **54.** TNA, E 179/346. **55.** TNA, C 5/27/85; Pettiward rent book 1669-70, in possession of Michael Bull; TNA, C 11/22/55. **56.** CWA, p. 272. **57.** LPL, VH 96/2525. **58.** Kesse in 1664. **59.** LPL, VH 96/946. **60.** WCR, Roll 149, 19 Oct 1658. **61.** LPL, VH 96/450. **62.** South and north have probably been reversed here. **63.** East Sussex RO, FRE 501. Rent later recorded as £20 pa in Wymondsold's notebook (NRO, Spencer books, 7j5, Surveys 12). **64.** TNA, PROB 11/216, Sir William Becher; G.E. Aylmer, *The King's servants* (1961), pp. 357, 366. **65.** Woodhead, p. 47. **66.** Poor in 1664 but a ratepayer in 1668. **67.** Mr Bosman was chargeable in 1664. **68.** QS, 1663-6, p. 214 (Jan 1665); 1668 rate. The 12 hearth figure is from the 1664 list, which records him as Mr John Roberts. Also 12 hearths in 1674. **69.** LPL, VH 96/688. **70.** QS, 1661-3, p. 70; TNA, C 24/908, Freeston v. Blount. **71.** WCR, 369/8, record of Wymondsold transfer 1685, No. 2. **72.** WCR, Roll 150, 30 Apr 1666. **73.** QS, 1663-6, p. 176. **74.** CWA, p. 537. **75.** Woodhead, p. 106. **76.** TNA, C 24/746, Handford v. Essington, evidence of Sir Thomas Dawes. **77.** TNA, C 24/661, Bradborne v. Wymondsold, p. 36. **78.** Woodhead, p. 71. **79.** *Ibid.*, p. 44. **80.** *Ibid.* **81.** Chargeable in 1662; omitted in 1664; paid rates in 1668; exempt in 1672. **82.** Woodhead, p. 129. **83.** WCR, 369/1, 6 Apr 1669. **84.** TNA, C 10/76/22. The lease was without entry fine. **85.** *Ibid.* **86.** *Ibid.* **87.** QS, 1663-6, p. 176. **88.** WCR, Roll 150, 30 Apr 1666. **89.** LPL, VH 96/1024. **90.** LMA, P95/MRY1/414, f. 1. **91.** The Hunt family later ran a nursery in Putney, though not on this site. **92.** QS, 1659-61, pp. 127, 132. See also WCR, Roll 149, 2 Apr 1657; QS, 1661-3, p. 185. **93.** CWA, p. 364. **94.** WCR, Roll 149, 2 Apr 1657; QS, 1661-3, p. 185. **95.** WCR, 369/2, 22 Dec 1675. **96.** WCR, Roll 150, 22 Apr 1664. **97.** Senior rather than junior because he was already living here in 1654 (WCR, Roll 147, Dec 1654). **98.** CWA, p. 509. **99.** LPL, VH 96/945. **100.** *Ibid.* **101.** TNA, PROB 11/334, James White. **102.** WCR, Roll 149, 19 Oct 1658. **103.** WLHS, list of payments by Putney overseers to watermen 1662-76. **104.** WCR, Roll 147, 6 Dec 1651. Lawson is recorded as 'Lacy' in 1663. **105.** LPL, VH 96/1537. **106.** LPL, VH 96/783. **107.** WCR, Roll 149, 28 Apr 1663, f. 18a. **108.** NA, PROB 24/10, f. 650. **109.** By then he was manager of Putney pottery. **110.** Friends' Library, Digest of Quaker births, book 840, p. 12. **111.** Williamson, p. 1144. **112.** LPL, VH 96/810. **113.** WCR, 369/5, 11 April 1687, Rogers to Pannett. **114.** WCR, Roll 149, m. 1a. **115.** CWA, p. 331; LMA, P95/MRY1/414, f. 132; register. **116.** Rogers is not mentioned in 1667, but is in 1688 as a former tenant (WCR, 369/5, 30 Apr 1688). **117.** V.B. Redstone (ed.), 'The diary of Sir Thomas Dawes, 1644', *Surrey Archaeological Collections*, vol. 37 (1927), p. 22. See also WCR, Roll 146, 1 Sept 1641; WCR, Roll 147, 23 Dec 1653. **118.** CWA, pp. 302, 313, 361. **119.** WCR, Roll 150, 30 Apr 1666. **120.** See Dorian Gerhold, *Villas and mansions of Roehampton and Putney Heath* (1997), p. 15. **121.** 1617 survey; WCR, Roll 143, 20 April 1615. **122.** LPL, VH 96/2738. **123.** TNA, PROB 4/796. **124.** *Ibid.* **125.** LPL, VH 96/409. Fire equipment is listed only for the red room and blue chamber. **126.** TNA, PROB 4/15195. **127.** TNA, C 24/881, Christopher v. Newstead. **128.** WCR, 369/6, 23 Apr 1694. For Munday and Norwood, see WCR 369/2, 30 April 1677. **129.** SHC, 176/2/5. **130.** *Ibid.* **131.** TNA, C 5/85/96; TNA, C 5/97/43. **132.** TNA, C 5/85/96; TNA, C 24/1412, Pettiward v. Bagnall, evidence of Susannah Hulke. **133.** TNA, PROB 4/12415. **134.** SHC, 176/2/8. **135.** TNA, PROB 11/338, Thomas Butler. **136.** WCR, 369/1, 4 May 1674, John Dawes. **137.** Lambeth Archives, deed 4765, 2nd schedule. The abuttals given in 1658 were repeated in the deed of 1860, though clearly incorrect. **138.** LPL, VH 96/2428. **139.** Friends Library, 11 b 15/7. **140.** SHC, 176/3/10; WCR, 369/5, 30 Apr 1699, Pettiward; both referring to James Magick. **141.** But also one rood with a tenement enclosed from David's Grove (just south from Downshire House), 1675 (SHC, 176/4/31, 1675 indenture). **142.** LPL, VH 96/1058. **143.** TNA, C 24/908, Freeston v. Blount. **144.** 1617 survey. **145.** WCR, 369/1, 4 May 1674, Cooper's lease. **146.** WCR, Roll 149, 1656. **147.** LPL, VH 96/2428. **148.** See Dorian Gerhold, *Roehampton village* (Wandsworth Paper, in preparation). **149.** TNA, C 24/925, Devonshire v. Bristol. **150.** CWA, p. 345. **151.** *Ibid.*, pp. 269, 313. The rent is not specifically stated as for a year. **152.** WCR, 369/2, 23 May 1676. **153.** QS, 1678-82, Easter 1680, p. 7. **154.** LPL, VH 97/3, p. 772; NRO, SOX 287, Man's lease 1747 and Horne's lease 1764. **155.** LPL, VH 96/1461. **156.** NRO, B(D)182. See Gerhold, *Roehampton village*. **157.** WCR, Roll 150, 30 Apr 1666. **158.** Leased out by Blunt (TNA, C 24/923, Blount v. Freeston), who had moved to Putney (No. 24). **159.** WCR, Roll 145, 5 May 1626.

Index

For an index of the householders of 1665, see pages 92-3.